Delicious.
The design & art direction of Stylorouge

Serving Suggestion

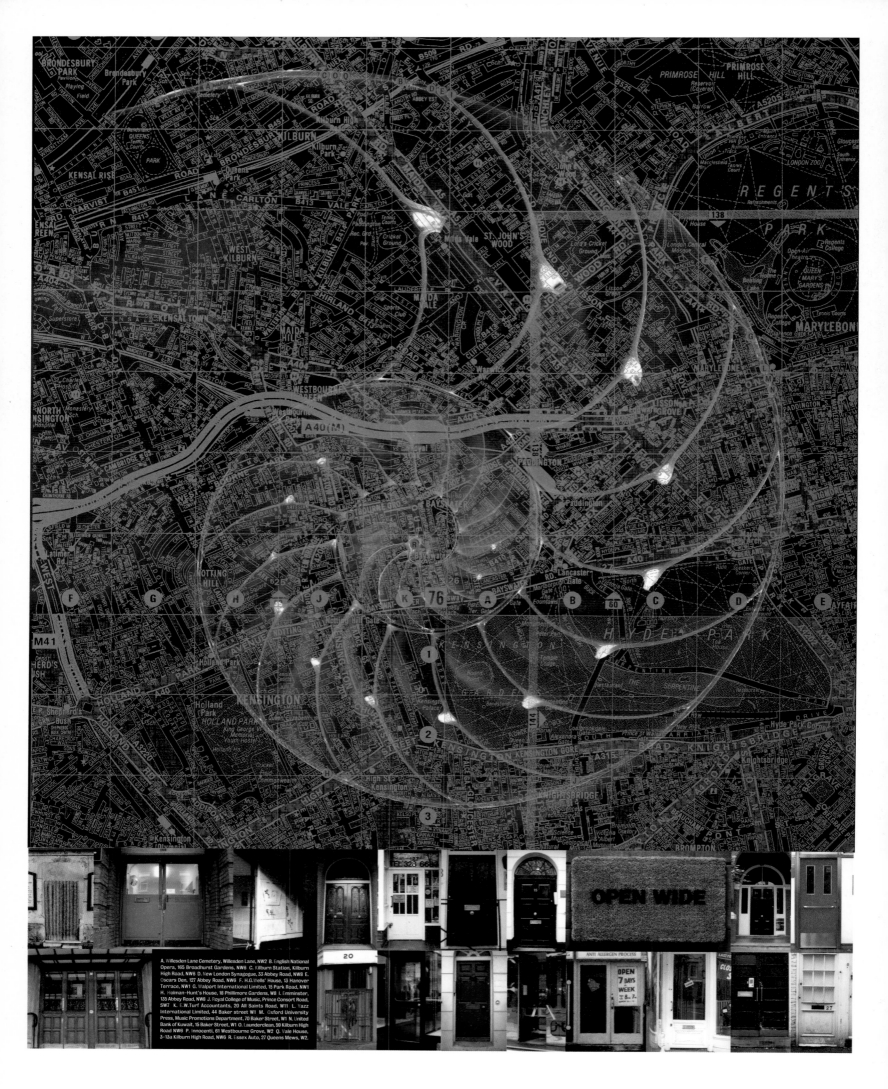

A. Willesden Lane Cemetery, Willesden Lane, NW2 B. English National Opera, 165 Broadhurst Gardens, NW6 C. Kilburn Station, Kilburn High Road, NW6 D. New London Synagogue, 33 Abbey Road, NW8 E. Oscars Den, 127 Abbey Road, NW8 F. H.G.Wells' House, 13 Hanover Terrace, NW1 G. Walport International Limited, 15 Park Road, NW1 H. Holman-Hunt's House, 18 Phillimore Gardens, W8 I. Emminster, 135 Abbey Road, NW8 J. Royal College of Music, Prince Consort Road, SW7 K. E.W.Turf Accountants, 20 All Saints Road, W11 L. Yazz International Limited, 44 Baker street W1 M. Oxford University Press, Music Promotions Department, 70 Baker Street, W1 N. United Bank of Kuwait, 15 Baker Street, W1 O. Launderclean, 59 Kilburn High Road NW6 P. Innocenti, 61 Westbourne Grove, W2 Q. Vale House, 3-13a Kilburn High Road, NW6 R. Essex Auto, 27 Queens Mews, W2.

by Jim Davies

There can't be many people who have survived 20 years in the music industry intact. It's a fickle, unforgiving business – what's considered the height of cool one day is decidedly passé the next. As well as artists, this rule applies to backroom personnel: producers; engineers; A&R people; management. And not least graphic designers. The visual aspect of popular culture is just as volatile as the aural. In photography, illustration and typography, trends shift just as radically or as subtly as in pop music and it takes instinct and adaptability to tap into the nuances of these changes.

When 25-year-old Rob O'Connor set up the design and art direction company Stylorouge in 1981, the national climate was grim. Two years into Margaret Thatcher's Draconian prime ministership, the country was in the grip of a recession. There were full-scale riots in Brixton, Toxteth in Liverpool, and the St Paul's area of Bristol. Ten protesters died in hunger strikes in Northern Ireland's Maze Prison. The miners were voicing their discontent, and Rupert Murdoch was tightening his grip on Times Newspapers and the unions. Stylorouge was established against this economic tide, opening for business when most of the news headlines were about closures.

In the more rarified world of graphic design, a quiet revolution was underway. Once dominated by the in-house design departments of the major record companies, a new, more radical aesthetic had developed in the aftermath of punk. T-shirts, record sleeves and fly posters became the most vibrant forms of graphic expression in the UK, steamrollering the fusty design 'rules' epitomised by the producers of airline liveries and annual reports. Freed from such corporate restraint, an uncompromising, expressive – and at times political – visual agenda had started to emerge.

It was in this context that O'Connor left the security of the art department of Polydor Records to go it alone. He named his design practice Stylorouge. This was chosen as a nod to his political leanings and in the spirit of the New Romantic period of the time. But it was mainly to disguise the fact that his 'company', was actually just himself and a drawing board housed in a small room above Capitelli's restaurant on London's Edgware Road.

O'Connor's old job took time to fill, so in the meantime he was able to continue developing relationships with Polydor artists on a freelance basis. These included Kirsty MacColl, Level 42, Siouxsie And The Banshees and Stiv Bators' new project, The Wanderers. But it wasn't long before the likes of A&M, Island and Chrysalis began commissioning him. After four months in business, O'Connor hired an old college friend Mick Lowe as a casual assistant, who eventually became Stylorouge's first full-time employee.

WILD THINGS BY THE CREATURES

DOUBLE 7" EP FEATURING: MAD EYED SCREAMER / SO UNREAL / BUT NOT THEM / WILD THING / THUMB PERFORMED BY SIOUXSIE SIOUX AND BUDGIE. AVAILABLE IN A LIMITED EDITION GATEFOLD PICTURE SLEEVE

Creatively, the highlight of the first year was O'Connor's ongoing collaboration with Siouxsie Sioux. A splinter group called The Creatures (featuring Siouxsie and her drummer/boyfriend Budgie) had been formed and required a visual identity that set them apart from the original Banshees.

For their debut Wild Things EP, O'Connor took up a suggestion from Siouxsie to develop a vaguely pornographic piece of illustrated mail from one of their more deviant fans. While The Creatures were on tour in Newcastle, a photo shoot was duly arranged in a cramped hotel bathroom. Adrian Boot took the photographs while O'Connor directed both the photos and the shower head. The resulting metallic black-and-white cover images, combined with the large, uncompromising sans type set on the vertical, still conveys a compelling seediness and sense of claustrophobia. Conceiving and executing such appropriate imagery was to become the guiding principle of Stylorouge.

For a designer, there's a major difference between working for a client that produces paper clips or dog food, and an artist who creates music. Or a film maker, novelist, or choreographer for that matter. In effect, your efforts become a representation of their creative endeavour and, on a more practical level, you need to learn how to deal with 'products' that live and breathe, have their own opinions and often answer back.

Around three-quarters of Stylorouge's design output is commissioned by the music industry, so the dilemma of satisfying client, artist and end-user crops up on a daily basis. In addition, the work must fulfil the designer's personal standards. No two jobs are alike. Debut singles need to be approached differently from fifth albums. An artist may be changing direction and want this reflected in his or her visual persona. The record label may want to appeal to a specific market sector. The band could be on the other side of the world on tour and unavailable for photography. And so it goes on.

The Creatures
Wild Things
EP Packaging

Siouxsie And The Banshees had played a charity afternoon show for Mencap so this was a night off. For The Creatures offshoot project Siouxsie and Budgie required a different look – something more human and physical.
These photographs were taken in a Newcastle hotel bathroom while other band members Steve Severin and John McGeogh watched Clash Of The Titans at a local cinema.

Orange Juice
Lean Period
7" Single

The record company usually has an agenda too, and it's essential for the designer to address this from an early stage. Often, bands have a well-defined idea of their image which may extend to printed or video-based promotional material. Before the design process even begins, they may have a full-blooded vision of what they want on the cover of their new album. Worse still, they may have artistic pretensions themselves — or even a boyfriend or girlfriend who fancy themselves with paintbrush or camera. With so many interested parties pulling in different directions, strength of personality and communication skills become an important part of the designer's make-up.

Having said that, flexibility and open-mindedness are also essential attributes. This dispassionate approach lies at the heart of Stylorouge's design philosophy. Each project is judged on its own merits, with different criteria applied accordingly. Appropriateness often takes precedent over personal style. Every project, from Mozart to Killing Joke to Blur, is approached with this attitude, without musical prejudice. The one constant is a respect for the image as the basis for all graphic communication.

It's difficult to say whether such an impartial, objective attitude has helped or hindered Stylorouge's profile over the years. While contemporaries have established instantly recognisable personal signatures, which have brought kudos and notoriety, Stylorouge has remained relatively anonymous. Certainly, Stylorouge's preferred design aesthetic has never competed with the visual persona of any of the bands it services — a conflict that would be self-defeating.

Any apparent lack of recognition can also be attributed to the company's collective mentality. All work is credited to Stylorouge rather than an individual or team, so a broad stylistic range of work is produced under the one banner. Design personnel have come and gone over the years (though many have stayed), bringing individual skills to the mix, affecting the dynamic of the studio and the direction of the work.

It's easy to see how Stylorouge's attitudes and working methods produce such startlingly different results. From the scratchy, homespun style created for singer-songwriter Mundy, to the slick, bleached-out cover for Geri Halliwell's debut album; the clean, knowing graphic language used for Blur's early recordings, to the cluttered, hippyesque world constructed for psychedelic popsters Kula Shaker. O'Connor constantly refers to the word 'personality', as if he feels the sleeve designer's quest is to eke out the inner psyche of the artist. Work from outside the entertainment industries has consistently come the company's way, but the designers have still sought to express a sense of personality, even when the job lacks a central human element.

"The reason so many people are drawn to this area of design," says O'Connor, "is because in the end it's selling something interesting, something worthwhile. It's not cigarettes or confectionery. There's an artistic integrity to it, even if it is often only pop music. Designers tend to have a natural empathy with the creative arts." And, despite all the various restrictions and pressures, it still offers the opportunity to be more creative and adventurous than most.

One of the most challenging aspects of the discipline is that it is constantly evolving. It can be affected by movements in the cultural landscape as it was in the post-punk era, as well as by developments in technology, as has become apparent more recently. Smaller music delivery systems, such as the CD, MiniDisc and now MP3, which does away with packaging altogether, mean that companies like Stylorouge are constantly having to adapt and reinvent themselves to survive and prosper. It's not a case of hankering over the 'good old days' of design for print, but trying to redirect the creative focus and core values into new exciting channels as media converge. Hardly surprisingly, Stylorouge has become increasingly involved in video production and web site design in recent years.

Having said that, Delicious is an unapologetic visual record of 20 years worth of design for print. It covers an array of styles from the elaborate to the minimal, the slick to the faux-naïve and everything in between. What's most remarkable is just how much of the design actually stands the test of time. And that's a testament to the power of the rigorous design idea, something that's always been at the heart of Stylorouge.

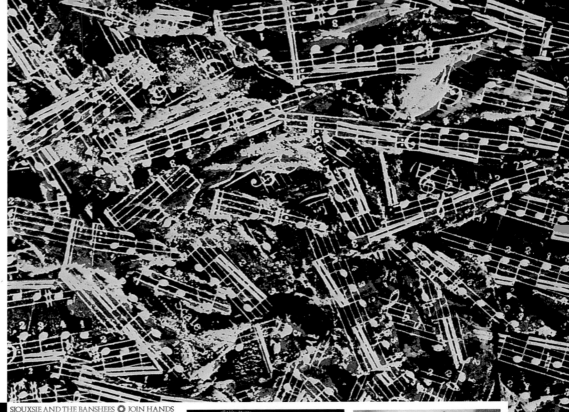

Bob Marley
Collection
Album Box set

Siouxsie And The Banshees
Join Hands
Album

The Wanderers
Only Lovers Left Alive
Album

The Chords
Maybe Tomorrow
Single

MAIN PICTURE
Siouxsie And The Banshees
juju
Album

Early Years

by Rob O'Connor

Illustrated by three diagrams of guitar-chord shapes, the ad in NME read, "This is a chord; here is another; and another. Now start a band". I believe it was intended to announce the release of the new single by punk group The Adverts, but it served as a suitable ethic for the time. The message was audacious and exciting – less rationalisation, more action – a 'Just Do It' for the so-called Blank Generation. The youthful swagger engendered by the spirit of punk was pervasive. If you wanted to do it then you could – musician, stylist, video director, fashion designer, art director; stick it on your CV (probably under an assumed new wave *nom de plume*) and away you went (quite possibly to the employment exchange to sign on). The point was that youthful creativity defied probability and thrived in this most hostile of social climates. In the UK the recession trudged on, businesses foundered but the punky reggae party would go on forever.

The inevitable happened, of course, and the major record companies attempted to bottle the zeitgeist by signing bands with more spit and spirit than skill; gaggles of satin tour jackets at the back of the Vortex betraying the A&R presence like a city gent on a British Rail football special. One such band caught in the net kicking and screaming were Siouxsie And The Banshees; Self-confessed musically untrained art school types from suburbia, their 20-minute live set landed them a deal with Polydor Records, joining a reviving roster which included other recent arrivals, The Jam, Sham 69 and punk poet Patrik Fitzgerald. Polydor's early Seventies profile had been kept afloat by Slade, Lyndsey de Paul and The Rubettes. How archaic and alien – indeed how pointless – these bubblegum careers now seemed.

I had just stumbled into a job in Polydor's art department. Six months out of art college, a modicum of talent, a voraciously unhealthy appetite for music and a little of that youthful swagger had paid dividends. For the first two or three days I toyed with the idea of being starstruck, but somehow it never kicked in properly. Even when Paul Weller visited Polydor's Stratford Place offices to accept his esteemed record company's congratulations for yet another number one chart entry – this time for Eton Rifles. He was preceded by his father and manager John announcing Paul's arrival like some bellowing MC at a boxing bout, besuited and swollen with pride.

The fact is, the likes of Siouxsie, Robert Smith and Jimmy Pursey seemed no different from my friends at school and art college – they just wanted to make music their living. In my capacity as an in-house designer I was happy to ply my own trade by packaging and advertising their output.

My first photo session came after only a month – it was a baptism of fire. Having given up on finding a visual direction that was acceptable to John Otway for his first solo album cover, I inherited the ill-fated project from my colleagues. John insisted we develop his girlfriend's idea, which involved a red Morris Minor, a map, a blue sports car and an English summer's day. It was February.

Otway's native Buckinghamshire was to form the backdrop for her vision; open, cold, wet and misty. John's choice of photographer was approved by the label manager. Even though his background was as a paparazzo, he was untrained in location work and had never used a medium-format camera, which Polydor insisted upon.

We tracked down an old convertible Morris and the manager of Polydor's vehicle fleet arranged for our lease company to provide the swish sports job. It was delivered to our offices early on the morning of the shoot. Brand new. 24 miles on the clock (I'll remember that figure forever). "Bend it, and I'll bend you," threatened the fleet manager (funny, I'll remember that forever as well). I was to drive this car and meet Otway and his band near the location in Lower Missenden. I arrived on time. So far, so good. We found the photographer setting up a tripod by the side of the road at the pre-arranged spot. He had no assistant, no location vehicle and just a handful of rolls of film. His hands were so cold that he had to wear thick woollen gloves throughout. Otway shivered visibly in his shirt sleeves, waiting patiently for the photographer's fumbling fingers and passing grey clouds, pretending that it was warm and sunny. Eventually, we turned our attention to shots of the less-patient band members who were to appear in the girlfriend's 'punchline' photo on the back of the album.

When the final shot had been taken, the juvenile idiot posing as a band member who happened to be behind the wheel of the brand new MG, decided to drive it up a country lane and into a ploughed field. It naturally became stuck, the churning wheels burying it nicely to about headlight level in the mud. (Strangely my idea of designing record sleeves hadn't accounted for situations such as this.)

We managed to free the car and I broke my journey home to spend the best part of an hour hosing it down in the darkness of a service station forecourt with the help of my passenger, Otway's drummer. Fortunately it was still predominantly blue under the brown.

The next afternoon I took receipt of about ten rolls of almost clear transparency film. All of them were horrifyingly over-exposed – none of them had been clip-tested – and I was faced with several options: resignation (a bit premature?); murder (mass); suicide (reluctant). I opted for tea and a wave of a white flag through my boss's door.

The job was saved by a gifted retoucher who as good as re-painted the whole image over an emaciated print. Gladly, we

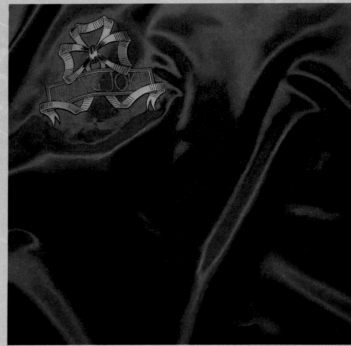

were able to laugh about the experience when I had the nervous pleasure of working with the same photographer some years later. Needless to say, the resulting design doesn't feature in these pages. I have tried to forget some of the similar horror stories that have happened since, but you always remember the first time you were screwed don't you?

By spring 1981, it felt like time to move on. I was not a comfortable company man and I desired a greater level of creative expression and income, both of which freelance status would offer me. In May that year Stylorouge took its first hesitant steps. For several months I worked alone but when the workload exceeded my sense of humour I engaged help and we began a slow steady growth; the increase in personnel enlightening me to the creative possibilities that result from working as a team. Collaboration would become a watchword for our approach to design. We thrived on exploring the potential of each new job – here we were with so many creative minds to meet and work with – musicians, actors, directors, photographers, illustrators, writers – so much ahead of us, so much yet to learn…

The Stranglers
European Female
Single

Iain Sutherland
Mixed Emotions
Album

Sham 69
The First The Best
And The Last
Album

Wham!
Bad Boys
Single

Killing Joke
Ha
Mini Album

Adam Ant
Vive le Rock
Album

OPPOSITE
Killing Joke
Sanity
Single

KILLING JOKE SANITY

THE NEW SINGLE ON SEVEN TWELVE COMPACT DISC

THE PASSIONS

I'M IN LOVE WITH A GERMAN FILM STAR

SHRIEKBACK

FISH BELOW THE ICE

Shriekback
Fish Below The Ice
Single

Music For Pleasure
Light
Single

Music For Pleasure
Time
Single

Music For Pleasure
Into The Rain
Album

OPPOSITE
The Passions
I'm In Love With A
German Film Star
Poster for single

Siouxsie and the Banshees
Israel
Single

Siouxsie and the Banshees
Spellbound
Poster for single

Siouxsie and the Banshees
Christine
Single

Scott Walker
Tilt
Album Packaging

A photo-illustrative composite
image of a blade, a cockerel and
Scott's own hands. A dark vision
based on the theme of one of the
album's key tracks 'The
Cockfighter'

Echo & The Bunnymen
Rust
Single Packaging

OPPOSITE
Wildflowers
The New York Jazz Loft
Sessions
Album Packaging

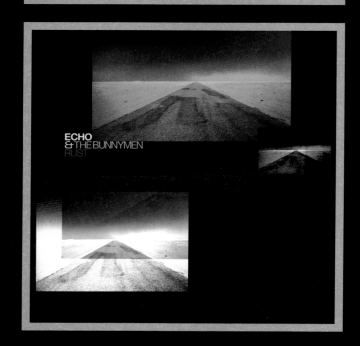

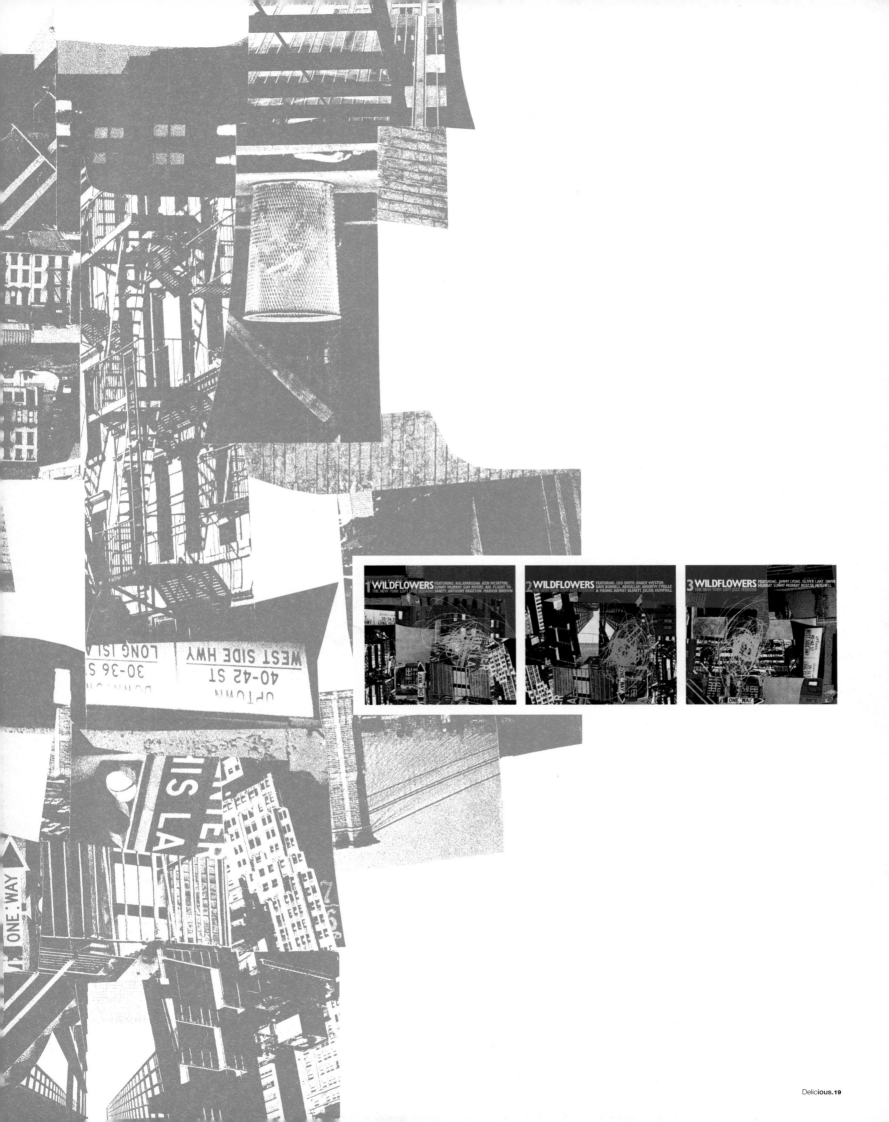

Salad
I Want You
Poster for single

OPPOSITE
Soul ll Soul
Represent
Single packaging

Each format of the single featured
the face over a different coloured
cross, provoking a range of instant,
and possibly misleading reactions.
An invitation to question our
preconceptions for one of the UK's
most actively anti-racist musicians.

I WANT YOU

THE NEW SINGLE BY SALAD OUT NOW WITH FIVE EXCLUSIVE NEW TRACKS CD 1 I WANT YOU DECADE OF THE BRAIN UGLY FASHION TOWN
CD 2 I WANT YOU ONE IN THE BAG A SIZE MORE WOMAN THAN HER 7" I WANT YOU FLY IN A SHEET OF WINTER

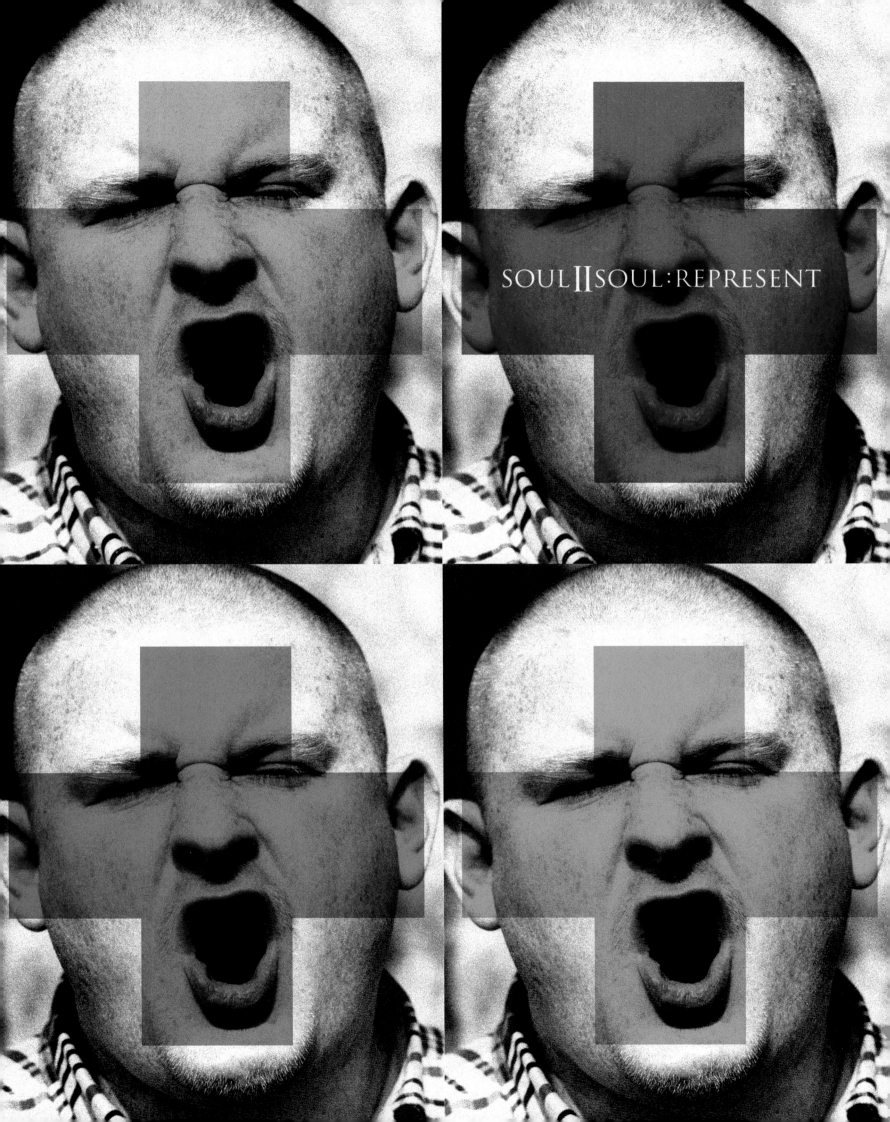

SOUL II SOUL:REPRESENT

'Corporate dinosaurs who throw up cyber-joneses should make their de effort - it's a visual and interactive de etentive and Netphobic MD"

Stylorouge
Perestroika
Pages from the website and frames
from the screensaver.

websites just to keep up with the
signers study this cutting-edge
light. Force-feed it to your anally

(seven)

"stranger than fiction"

A NEW SINGLE ON 7"AND EXTENDED 12"

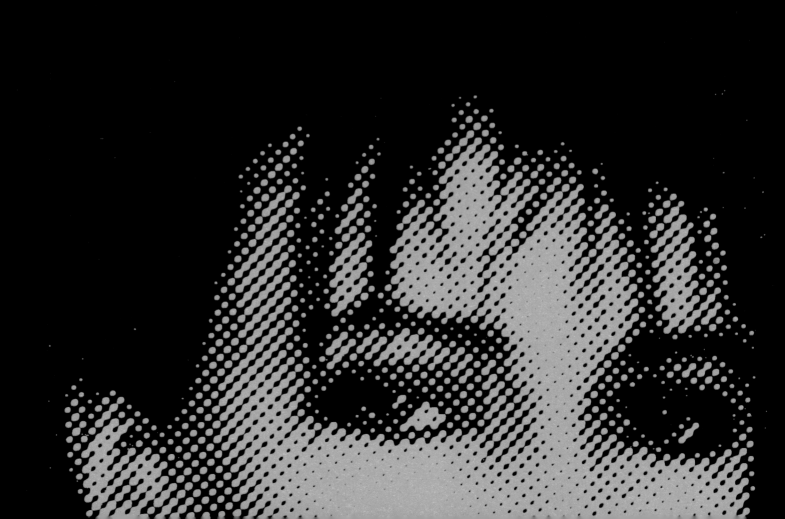

Nik Kershaw
The Works
Album

Lili Marleen
Soundtrack
Album

OPPOSITE
Inge Van Hendrick
Switch Me On
Album

All At Once

Inge van Hendrick
Switch Me On

Stylorouge
Self promotional
postcards
Vaccuum-packed book, cover
and inside pages

_310
_x
_240
_mm

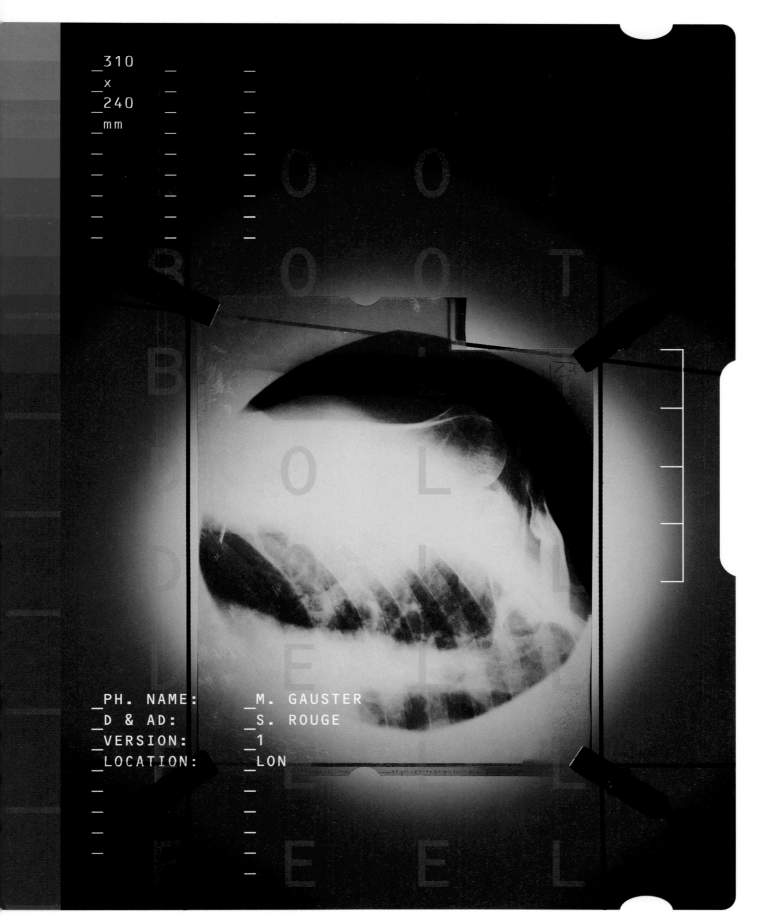

_PH. NAME: _M. GAUSTER
_D & AD: _S. ROUGE
_VERSION: _1
_LOCATION: _LON

Baby Chaos
Ignoramus
Single

OPPOSITE
The Passions
Thirty thousand feet over China
Poster for album

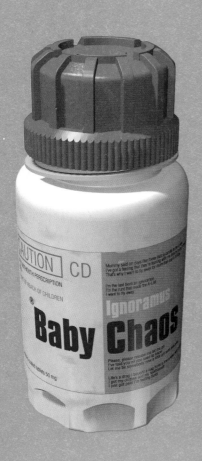

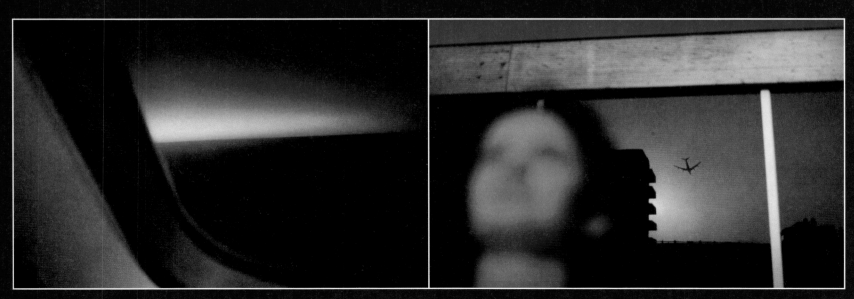

dot.cam

NARROWBAND INTERACTIVE VIDEO-WEBCAMS

abcdefghijklmnopqrstuuwxyz
1234567890.,:;"&!?
hamburger istiu fam admodum mitigati raptarum animi erant sed earum
parentes rum maxime sordida ueste lacrimisque et querelis ciuitates

>>www.coppernob.com

THE ARTS CLINIC

The Arts Clinic
Corporate identity and
leaflet spreads

OPPOSITE
Coppernob
Corporate identity, advertising,
website and font design for
lifestyle/retail brand.
A complete re-appraisal of
visual identity for the UK- based
fashion label.

for creative minds

THE ARTS CLINIC...makes it better.

THE ARTS CLINIC
★ ☎ (+44) 0171 935 1242 ✚

14 Devonshire Place, London W1N 1PB
fax (+44) 0171 224 6256
e-mail: mail@artsclinic.co.uk
www.artsclinic.co.uk

Profits down? - **Get Creative Mentoring
NOW** • Delivering the goods?- **Access The
Creative Dynamic** • Band / Group /
Department conflict - **Group Dynamics Work**
• Short on confidence? - **Let's Build It** • Poor
performance? - **Get Results** • Unmanageable
managers? - **We'll Show You How** • don't
know where to start? - **Get In Training** •
Doing well? - **Do Even Better** • Already big?
- **Get Massive** • Creative block? - **Blast It!** •
Drugs and alcohol dependence? - **We Can
Sort It** • Difficult artists? - **Practical Solutions**

THE ARTS CLINIC....

makes it better

Our service is **confidential** *and* **discreet** *acknowledging at all times the sensitive nature of the work involved.*

"...raw-boned realism, red in tooth and claw, that gets as

HAMBUR

Hamburger Hill
Film Poster

In May 1969, American forces on a search and destroy operation fought in one of the fiercest engagements of the Vietnam war, suffering many terrible casualties (hence the name). Hundreds of American soldiers died at Hamburger Hill – a fact that was very well publicised in the American media. A month later, after the American forces withdrew from the area to continue operations elsewhere, the hill was reoccupied by the North Vietnamese army.

The movie Hamburger Hill, was one of the most disturbingly violent of all the Vietnam movies made. Rather than exploit this fact, and risk glamourising the horror, the poster used an image of a single figure, looking vulnerable and defeated.

The helicopters were added at the client's request to reinforce the Vietnam image.

"...raw-boned realism, red in tooth and claw, that gets as

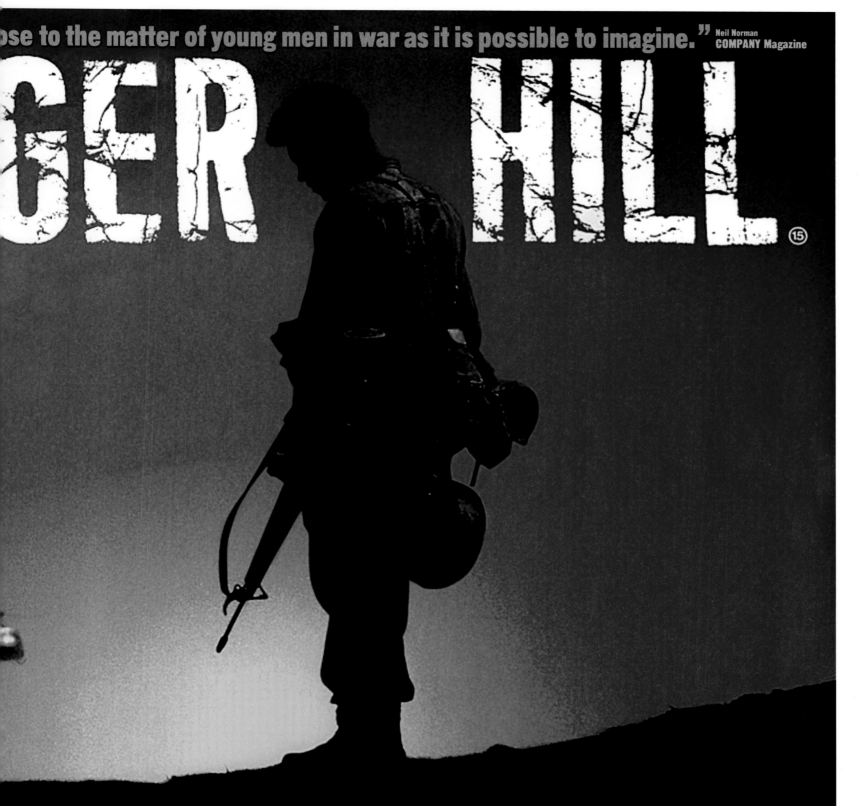

"...ose to the matter of young men in war as it is possible to imagine." Neil Norman COMPANY Magazine

GER HILL ⑮

WAR AT ITS WORST
FOUGHT BY YOUNG MEN AT THEIR BEST

RKO PICTURES AND INTERACCESS FILM DISTRIBUTION PRESENTS A MARCIA NASATIR AND JIM CARABATSOS PRODUCTION
A JOHN IRVIN FILM HAMBURGER HILL Original Music By PHILIP GLASS
Executive Producers JERRY OFFSAY and DAVID KORDA Co-Produced by LARRY DE WAAY Written By JIM CARABATSOS
Produced by MARCIA NASATIR and JIM CARABATSOS Directed By JOHN IRVIN
Production Facilities and Service Furnished by General Film Productions Philippines, Inc.
A PALACE PICTURES Release

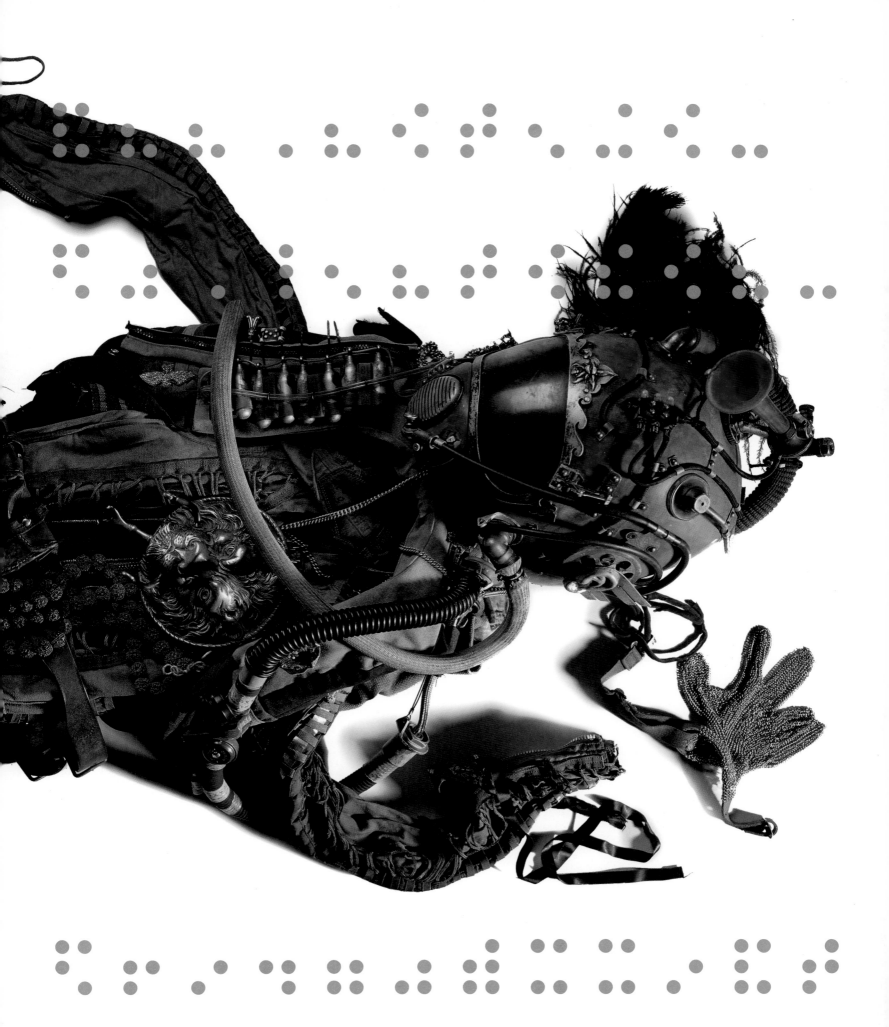

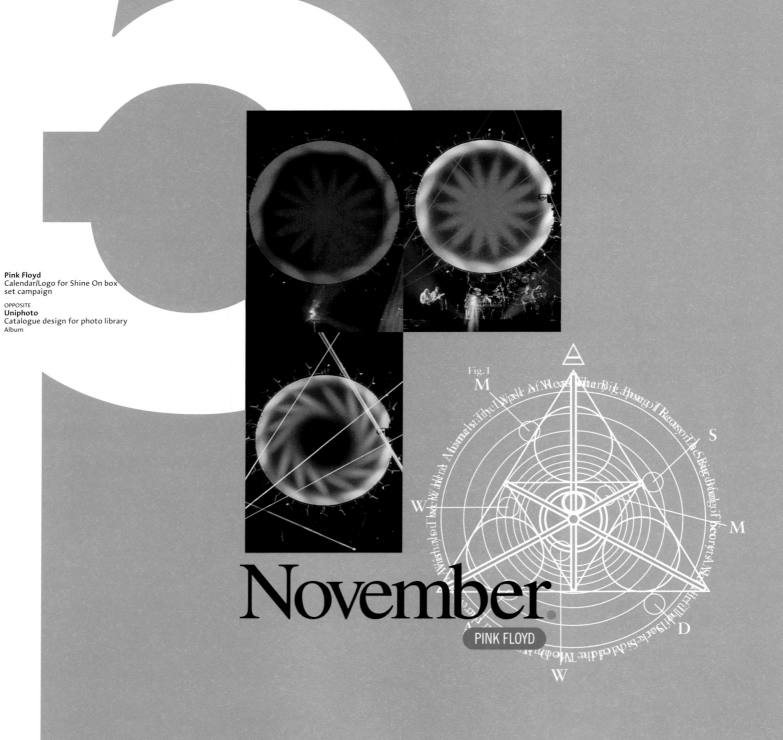

Pink Floyd
Calendar/Logo for Shine On box
set campaign

OPPOSITE
Uniphoto
Catalogue design for photo library
Album

November.

PINK FLOYD

Fig.1

UNIPHOTO 10

Straw
Keepsakes
Proposal for album sleeve

OPPOSITE
Baby Chaos
Love your self abuse
Album

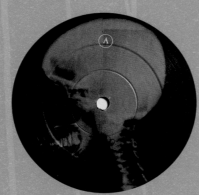

Label designs for:

Nik Kershaw
One Step Ahead

Blur
The Great Escape

Menswear
Stardust

Raw Stylus
Single

Regal
Promo

Mundy
Pardon Me

Kula Shaker
303

Baby Chaos
Safe Sex Designer
Drugs And The Death
Of Rock 'N' Roll

Twin Town
Soundtrack

Mundy
Jelly Legs

Baby Chaos
Hello

Regal
Promo

Catatonia
Road Rage

Glasgow Gangster Funktracs
Deeva Feeva

Prefab Sprout
Andromeda Heights

Raw Stylus
Pushing Against The Flow

Sleeper
Delicious

Baby Chaos
Golden Tooth

Dawn Of Electronica
Compilation album

Jesus Jones
Perverse
Album packaging

A voyeuristic series of photographs progressively revealing more of a story as the viewpoint recedes. Shot in a family home in Southwest London.
Not the most interesting of the images, but carrying the most immediate marketing impact, a raw photocopied re-creation of a close-up (opposite) became the front cover.
The Mexican-style wrestlers were played by Putney gym members, the girls by the stylist and the make-up artist respectively.

Regal Recordings
House bag
Promo wallet

OPPOSITE
Regal Recordings
Corporate identity
(Reverse of letterhead shown)

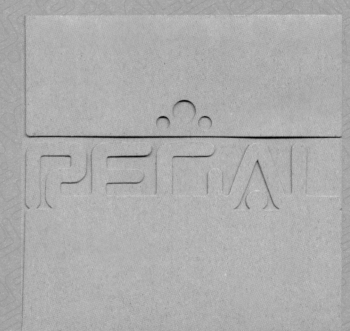

CUSACK
GOODMAN

WHAT PRICE JUSTICE?

THE JACK BULL

HBO PICTURES PRESENTS A NEW CRIME PRODUCTION IN ASSOCIATION WITH RIVER ONE FILMS A JOHN BADHAM FILM JOHN CUSACK JOHN GOODMAN "THE JACK BULL" L.Q. JONES MIRANDA OTTO JOHN C. McGINLEY JOHN SAVAGE JAY O. SANDERS AND SCOTT WILSON MUSIC BY LENNIE NIEHAUS EDITOR FRANK MORRISS PRODUCTION DESIGNER RICK ROBERTS DIRECTOR OF PHOTOGRAPHY GALE TATTERSALL PRODUCED BY KEVIN REIDY CO-PRODUCER D.V. DeVINCENTIS EXECUTIVE PRODUCERS JOHN CUSACK, STEVE PINK, JOHN C. McGINLEY, THOMAS J. MANGAN IV WRITTEN BY DICK CUSACK INSPIRED BY THE BOOK ENTITLED "MICHAEL KOHLAAS" BY HEINRICK VON KLEIST DIRECTED BY JOHN BADHAM

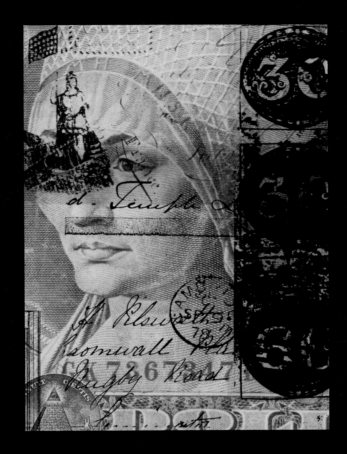

Conspiracy
Proposal for Album packaging

OPPOSITE
The Jack Bull
Film poster

Desert Eagle Discs
The Lovers
'images for single'

OPPOSITE
Desert Eagle Discs
Would You Kill for Me?
'images for single'

LOCATION WOOLWICH FOOT TUNNEL
POSTAL DISTRICT SE18 6DL
CONDITIONS COLD
DATE NOVEMBER 1999

LOCATION CAMLEY STREET
POSTAL DISTRICT NW1 1UU
CONDITIONS HOT
DATE DECEMBER 1999

Heather Small
Proud
Album

OPPOSITE
Sandie Shaw
Frederick
Image from single

24 Seven
Brand design and packaging
Developed for a range of body sprays
targeted at the young male market

OPPOSITE
Stylorouge
Home
T shirt

Home: Indigo Bloom, Velvet Peach, Sour Cream Creme, Bardot Blue, Paracetamol White, Caramel Blush, Kingfisher Glow, Zanzibar Lavender, Rhodamine Rouge, Stetson Sage, Terracotta Fudge, Montenegro Twilight, Emmerdale Dawn, Chipshop Blue, Sistine Citron, Weimaraner Mousse, Dartford Blonde, Velasquez Beige, Loganberry Pavanne, Coffee Velour, Creole Lily, Hughie Green, Salem Tartan, Custard Cream, Magnolia. **Stylorouge.**

1 daydreamer		
2 i'll manage somehow	produced by marc waterman	design by stylorouge
3 sleeping in	published by island music	℗1996 laurel. ©1996 laurel. laurel: po box 2400, london nw10 5ne the copyright in this sound recording is owned by laurel records
4 being brave		

Mansun
Tax Loss
CD single label

OPPOSITE
Menswear
Daydreamer
Single
I'll Manage Somehow
Single
Sleeping In
Single
Being Brave
Single

CATATONIA
INTERNATIONAL VELVET

Catatonia
International Velvet
Album front and back

OPPOSITE
Voice of the Beehive
Sex & Misery
Album

1 MULDER AND SCULLY
2 GAME ON
3 I AM THE MOB
4 ROAD RAGE
5 JOHNNY COME LATELY
6 GOLDFISH AND PARACETAMOL
7 INTERNATIONAL VELVET
8 WHY I CAN'T STAND ONE NIGHT STANDS
9 PART OF THE FURNITURE
10 DON'T NEED THE SUNSHINE
11 STRANGE GLUE
12 MY SELFISH GENE

Lighthouse Family Postcard From Heaven

[1]Raincloud [2]Once In A Blue Moon [3]Question Of Faith [4]Let It All Change [5]Sun In The Night [6]High [7]Lost In Space [8]When I Was Younger [9]Restless [10]Postcard From Heaven

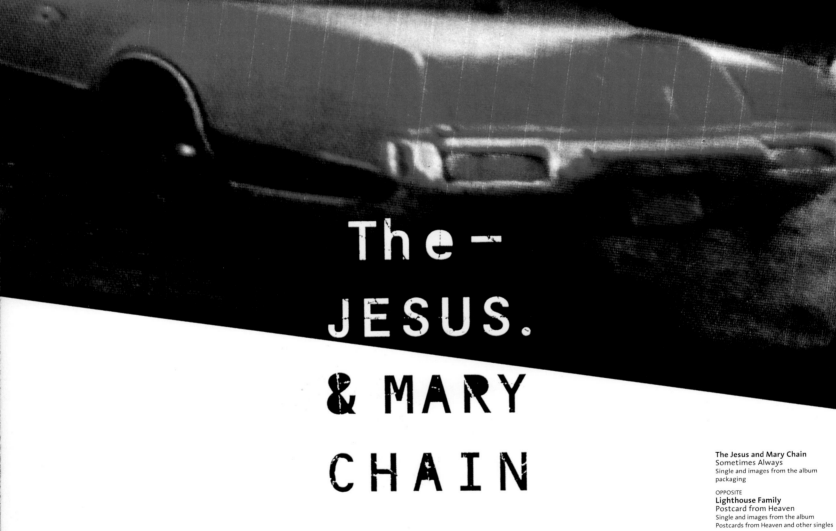

The — JESUS. & MARY CHAIN

SOMETIMES ALWAYS

The Jesus and Mary Chain
Sometimes Always
Single and images from the album
packaging

OPPOSITE
Lighthouse Family
Postcard from Heaven
Single and images from the album
Postcards from Heaven and other singles

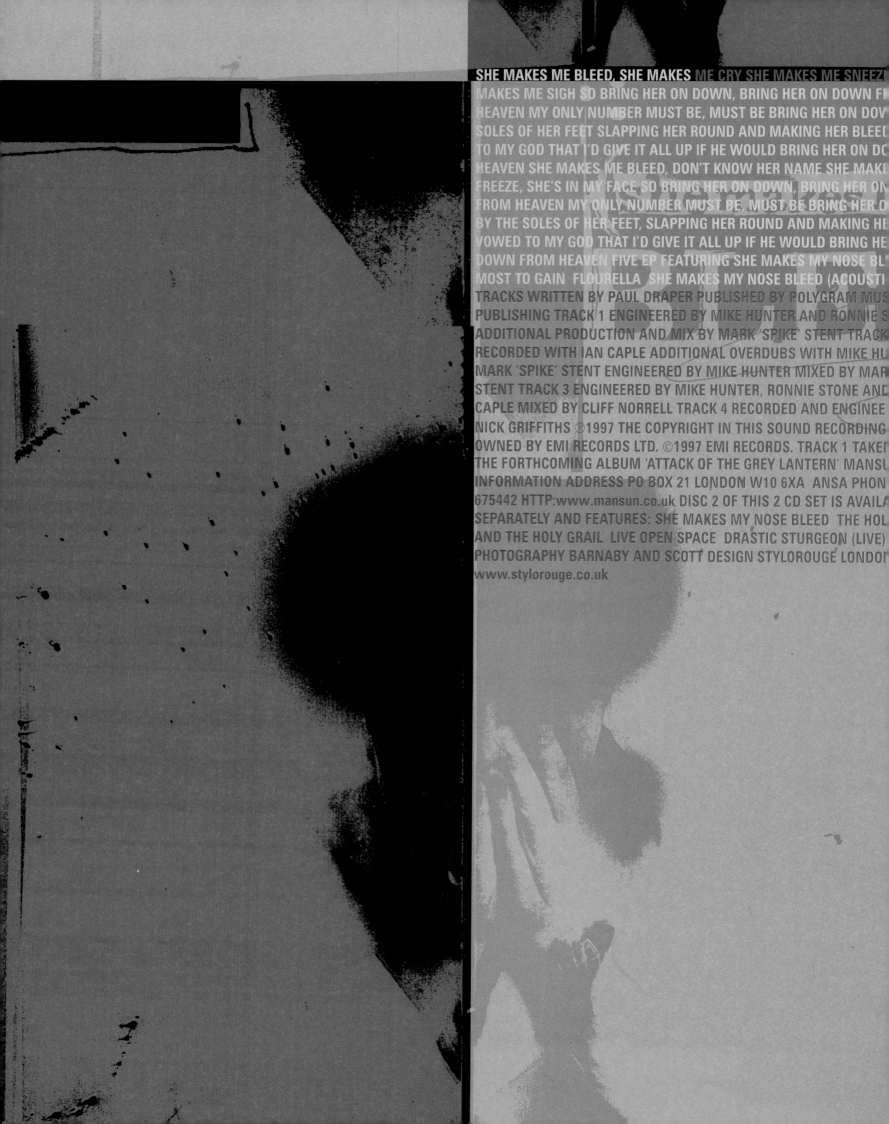

SHE MAKES ME BLEED, SHE MAKES ME CRY SHE MAKES ME SNEEZE
MAKES ME SIGH SO BRING HER ON DOWN, BRING HER ON DOWN FR
HEAVEN MY ONLY NUMBER MUST BE, MUST BE BRING HER ON DOV
SOLES OF HER FEET SLAPPING HER ROUND AND MAKING HER BLEED
TO MY GOD THAT I'D GIVE IT ALL UP IF HE WOULD BRING HER ON DO
HEAVEN SHE MAKES ME BLEED, DON'T KNOW HER NAME SHE MAKI
FREEZE, SHE'S IN MY FACE SO BRING HER ON DOWN, BRING HER ON
FROM HEAVEN MY ONLY NUMBER MUST BE, MUST BE BRING HER O
BY THE SOLES OF HER FEET, SLAPPING HER ROUND AND MAKING HE
VOWED TO MY GOD THAT I'D GIVE IT ALL UP IF HE WOULD BRING HE
DOWN FROM HEAVEN FIVE EP FEATURING SHE MAKES MY NOSE BL'
MOST TO GAIN FLOURELLA SHE MAKES MY NOSE BLEED (ACOUSTI
TRACKS WRITTEN BY PAUL DRAPER PUBLISHED BY POLYGRAM MUS
PUBLISHING TRACK 1 ENGINEERED BY MIKE HUNTER AND RONNIE S
ADDITIONAL PRODUCTION AND MIX BY MARK 'SPIKE' STENT TRACK
RECORDED WITH IAN CAPLE ADDITIONAL OVERDUBS WITH MIKE HU
MARK 'SPIKE' STENT ENGINEERED BY MIKE HUNTER MIXED BY MAR
STENT TRACK 3 ENGINEERED BY MIKE HUNTER, RONNIE STONE AND
CAPLE MIXED BY CLIFF NORRELL TRACK 4 RECORDED AND ENGINEE
NICK GRIFFITHS ℗1997 THE COPYRIGHT IN THIS SOUND RECORDING
OWNED BY EMI RECORDS LTD. ©1997 EMI RECORDS. TRACK 1 TAKEI
THE FORTHCOMING ALBUM 'ATTACK OF THE GREY LANTERN' MANSU
INFORMATION ADDRESS PO BOX 21 LONDON W10 6XA ANSA PHON
675442 HTTP:www.mansun.co.uk DISC 2 OF THIS 2 CD SET IS AVAILA
SEPARATELY AND FEATURES: SHE MAKES MY NOSE BLEED THE HOL
AND THE HOLY GRAIL LIVE OPEN SPACE DRASTIC STURGEON (LIVE)
PHOTOGRAPHY BARNABY AND SCOTT DESIGN STYLOROUGE LONDOI
www.stylorouge.co.uk

Menswear
Menswear
Nuisance
Album
OPPOSITE
Mansun
She Makes my Nose Bleed
Single

LONGPIGS
>MOBILE HOME

Longpigs
The Frank Sonata/Blue Skies
Singles and selected images

OPPOSITE
Longpigs
Mobile Home
Album

The chosen shot from a two day
jaunt through various parts of Los
Angeles, following our anonymous
actor/model and his unlikely
companion.
After several weeks of indecision
within the band about the other
visuals we had presented we
finally got the perfect brief - "you
know the title, do what *you* want
to do".
Part of the shoot took place on
the flat roof of a photographic
hire studio, the cheapest space in
the complex. We visited the day
before the shoot to check it out
and discovered the Airstream
trailer, which stood there
permanently as a changing room.
The abstracted theme we were
developing through the use of the
fish was of displacement, but
bearing in mind the album title,
we used the trailer in the shots
despite the literal reference. It
would have seemed somewhat
perverse not to.

Food
The Food Christmas EP 1989
EP

James
Wah Wah
Proposal for album

OPPOSITE
Prick Up Your Ears
Video Inlay (front and back)

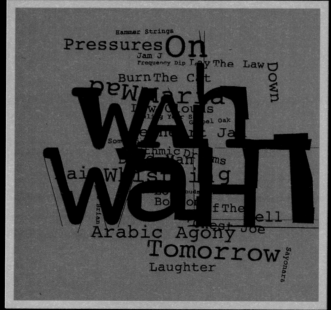

KENNETH.

Prick up your ears

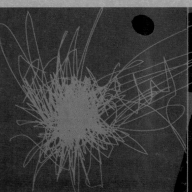

120x240

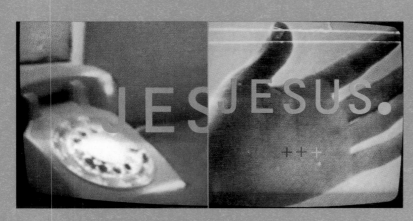

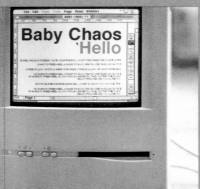

Miki Imai
Pride
Album

PRIDE

MIKIIMAI

Menswear
We Love You
Single

MENSWEAR

WE LOVE YOU ²·CRASH ³·PHAT KID MUSIC ⁴·HANG-
NG IN THE BLUE SKY ⁵·THE ONE* ⁶·SLEEPING IN*
LITTLE MISS PINPOINT EYES*ALL SONGS WRITTEN
BY DEAN/GENTRY/EVERITT/WHITE/BLACK/FLETCH-
ER. TRACKS 5,6 & 7 WRITTEN BY DEAN/GENTRY/
EVERITT/WHITE/BLACK. TRACK 1 PRODUCED BY
GUS DUDGEON. ENGINEERED BY LEIGH JEMISON
@ METROPOLIS STUDIOS. REMIXED BY ALAN
WINSTANLEY @ WESTSIDE STUDIOS. MIX ENGINEER
LEIGH JEMISON. 2,3 & 4 ENGINEERED BY LEIGH
JEMISON @ AOSIS/REWIND STUDIOS, LONDON.*5,6
& 7 RECORDED LIVE. ALL TRACKS PUBLISHED BY
SLAND MUSIC. DESIGN & ART DIRECTION BY
STYLOROUGE. PHOTOGRAPHY BY SIMON FOWLER
©1996 LAUREL ©1996 LAUREL. LAUREL: PO BOX
2400, LONDON NW10 5NF.

Look at Me

by Jim Davies

Since the advent of the microgroove vinyl record in 1949, the cover portrait has been the stock-in-trade of the record sleeve designer. Walk into any new-fangled record store during the 1950s and there they'd be: rack upon rack of quiffed crooners, dressed like knitwear pattern models, making eye contact and beseeching you to put your hand in your pocket. This overused design route took its cue from an earlier form of promotional art – the movie poster – which used the familiar features of Hollywood icons to great effect.

With movies, at least there's a rationale behind using images of leading actors to tout the product. After all, you see the same stars in ten-foot-high celluloid when you go to the cinema. Movie posters are a static taster, a fleeting impression of what you might expect to see after you buy your popcorn. But follow the same line of reasoning for records or CDs, and it would make more sense to produce a snatch of audio to advertise a forthcoming release rather than a use a contrived photograph of the man, woman or group of people who created it.

The promotional video, now such an integral part of the record industry marketing machinery, addresses this conundrum up to a point, presenting a more complex version of an artist's personality than a single still portrait. But how often have you heard the criticism that video diminishes the song for the listener, that the imagination is compromised by the director's imposed images? At best it can offer iconic status to a track and its performer. At worst it presents a false or crass image, and often exposes the artist's lack of performing ability.

It's quite ridiculous to believe that a simple snapshot of a musician can somehow suggest the essence of their music. A publisher wouldn't consider using an author's portrait on the front of a book cover to convey the contents of a novel, no matter how intriguing or soulful they looked. Fiction is a monument to the imagination, nothing to do with the composition of a face. Even so, the practice of plonking musicians on record

sleeves has become an industry standard, and often record company executives genuinely believe it's a commercial imperative. Faced with this constricting brief, graphic designers need to be imaginative and resourceful, stretching their ingenuity and skill to find new ways of distinguishing one pretty 20-something from another.

When an artist's face and music is familiar enough, perhaps you can excuse the head-and-shoulders format. If you saw a photograph of George Michael on a CD cover, for example, you might well anticipate a George Michael record. But even this is presumptuous. (The Wedding Present famously used a photo of football icon George Best, and Sonic Youth a detail of Madonna's face). You're basing your expectations on what has gone before. What if George is planning a change of direction? Say he's after a completely different groove from the last album?

When Stylorouge collaborated with George on his 1987 album Faith, he was looking to do just that – to produce a more sophisticated, adult sound. This was reflected in the grity side-on Russell Young photograph, where George, in distressed leather jacket, appears to be, well, sniffing his armpit. With hindsight, it's quite a camp image, but at the time it was taken very much at face value – intimate, introspective and moody. There was no type at all on the original front cover image (just a row of gold hieroglyphics drawn by George himself), a confident decision though, intriguingly, artist and title were added to subsequent reprints.

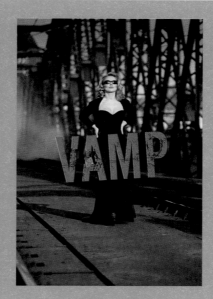
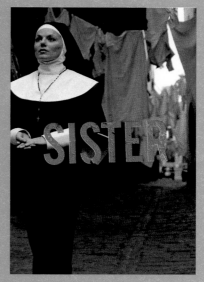

If you've no idea who an artist is, however, a cover photograph can mean next to nothing – you're left guessing what the sound might be like by appearance, clothes, photography and art direction.

If the subject on the cover is black you might anticipate soul or rap music, depending on how they are dressed. But again, you're speculating. It could just as easily be a jazz or rock record. Unfortunately, today's CD buyers have been conditioned to recognise musical genres by established visual clues, which encourages pigeonholing and can channel design solutions in predictable directions.

Good looks also send mixed signals. In the right context, a photograph of a high-cheekboned boy or pouting girl may well appeal purely on a sexual level, but to 'true' music lovers, physical perfection can raise suspicions. Pushing sex appeal may suggest packaging and contrivance – can this guy really sing or play? Does he rely on session musicians? Is he more than a pretty face?

Today's consumer is far more savvy about promotional trickery than their parents or grandparents. They recognise that the mug shot is a marketing-driven cliché, that the face peering from their CD is probably there at the insistence of the record company, or possibly the egotism of the artist, whether it works on a visual level or not. At worst, a full-on head-and-shoulders CD cover will be greeted with derision, at best as a post-modern joke. But more often than not it will be regarded as mere wallpaper – a missed opportunity perhaps, but no more than you'd expect.

With the blessing of Dave Balfe, then CEO of Food Records, Stylorouge's cover for Blur's Leisure album poked fun at the music industry's apparent obsession with the head-and-shoulders format, placing an extravagantly kitsch photograph of an anonymous woman in a bathing cap centre stage. Despite their indie darling looks, Blur have never actually appeared on any of their covers. This may seem perverse, but it was a deliberate tactical move, underlining their non-conformist credentials, a decision taken safe in the knowledge that their media profile would make up for it.

For many artists, however, cover portraits remain an integral part of the graphic vocabulary. Records aimed at the less sophisticated end of the visual market, chart-oriented pop for instance, are obvious candidates for this treatment. It's so-called 'role-model' marketing, where the audience identifies with and aspires to the values and cool, glamorous lifestyle of the artist. Mainstream MOR records aimed at mass-market consumers of tabloid newspapers and celebrity magazines like Hello and OK! pander to this format, as though it were the only visual language the market would understand.

But if, as a designer, you are 'encouraged' to feature an artist, there are countless different ways of going about it. One of the first record companies to exploit the possibilities was the jazz label Blue Note, which used smoky, atmospheric black-and-white shots by the photographer Francis Wolff on many of its ground-breaking covers. They depicted the label's impressive roster of artists as bona fide musicians, often capturing them in the heat of performance. No cheesy grins to threaten integrity here – these guys were artists, they were cool, the real McCoy.

The Beatles also took a progressive tack by employing fashion photographer Robert Freeman to shoot the portraits for their early sleeves. The 1964 album Beatles for Sale showed the band outside looking windswept and ruddy faced in black coats and scarves, a blur of red and green foliage in front of them. The title and photograph knowingly acknowledged the face as a sales tool.

As a designer, moving away from the constricting head-and-shoulders composition is always a good start. What can you do with such an uninspiring set-up, except rely on photographic trickery – perhaps throw it out of focus or play with the colour? But this is the real challenge – how to give a cover image of the artist an original look, a unique selling point. A Stylorouge cover for Mick Karn – former bassist with the 1980s band Japan – showed him stripped to the waist and smeared in what appeared to be thick, black motor oil, a radical departure from his immaculate contemporaries. On the face of it this idea seemed self-effacing, destructive even, given Karn's acknowledged good looks. But it

Adam Ant
Apollo 9
Poster for single

gave the image a sculptural quality, casting the subject as a living embodiment of art – apposite as Karn also happens to be a talented sculptor. And the overall effect was unnerving. Karn appeared bug-eyed and threatening, his eyes the only part of him free of make-up.

The back cover featured an altogether more passive portrait of the bassist, eyes closed, caked in flaking clay. This raises an interesting point. In this context, facial expression is all-important. The designer and photographer between them must decide what they are trying to convey about the artist and his music early on. Closed eyes can suggest an enigma or thoughtful demeanour, open eyes an invitation to the viewer, perhaps even a confessional honesty. Of course it depends on the particular eyes too – if you have eyes as unique as David Bowie's at your disposal, it's a sin not to use them. To smile, scowl or smoulder is another perennial question.

Placing the protagonist in an unusual setting is always worth considering. Photographer Andy Earl, a regular Stylorouge collaborator, often uses dramatic natural landscapes – beaches, dunes, cliffs, fields – to frame musicians. This serves to add a sense of intrigue – what are they doing? How did they get there? Does the location have some connection with the music? It also implies that the artist is alone with their thoughts or in their own real or imaginary habitat, that you're being allowed a glimpse of their unique world. The visual message is generally subliminal, you perceive colour, texture, atmosphere and associate them subconsciously with the music.

Musicians who are not so comfortable playing to the camera can still offer scope for creativity. Not everyone is prepared to expose themselves like Robbie Williams, but putting in a convincing performance can add spark to a portrait. For the 1984 single Apollo 9, photographed by Marc Lebon for Stylorouge, Adam Ant went outside the small Soho barbershop where the photo shoot was taking place in the early hours of the morning and did a couple hundred press ups on the pavement. Suitably pumped up, the resulting image has a powerful sense of aggression and

adrenalin. It is all too rare that an artist actually considers what they convey about themselves in their own image. Is there a story to tell, a feeling to evoke or a point to be made? This could be a once-in-a-lifetime situation. Surely you owe it to yourself to make this opportunity for self expression count.

With a close-up portrait, even the smallest facial gesture becomes exaggerated. A glint of the eye, a twitch of the mouth can become potent signifiers. But this is like reading meaning into a cashew nut. Unless you are a band like Kraftwerk, deliberately trading on a robotic aesthetic, paring a photograph down to its basics, placing a flawless face on a bland, bleached-out background adds nothing to the overall story. Rather than being enigmatic, it implies that the artist has nothing to say. Merely going through the motions of producing this kind of album cover picture can give the artist the look of an empty shell (the lights are on but there's nobody home).

Worse still are instances when an artist's true features are deliberately disguised. Flattering photography and digital retouching have become so over-used that in reality artists have come to bear little resemblance to their spruced-up promotional persona. Taking their cue from glossy magazines and press advertising, record sleeves seem to be telling us that we live in a world without skin blemishes, where everyone is slim, has luxuriant hair and no-one is dentally challenged. Eighties heart-throb Paul Young was known to have joked that it would probably cost his record company less to check him in for cosmetic surgery than to lay out for photographic retouching.

Of course there have been some iconic mug shots. Marvin Gaye on the cover of What's Going On, David Bowie on Aladdin Sane, The Ramones' eponymous LP, Bob Marley's Catch a Fire, T Rex's The Slider and U2's Joshua Tree. For every one of these, however, there have been literally thousands which have passed into obscurity. The portrait may be a legitimate design solution, but it's a decidedly limited one compared to the many alternative visual possibilities inside a designer's head.

"It is all too rare that an artist actually considers what they convey about themselves in their own image. Is there a story to tell, a feeling to evoke or a point to be made? This could be a once-in-a-lifetime situation. Surely you owe it to yourself to make this opportunity for self expression count."

Lena Fiagbe
Promotional photograph
Used on the packaging for Lena's album, this was one of a series of shots which examined her feelings regarding her image and ethnic roots

OPPOSITE
Angel Pie
She/Tin Foil Valley
Elements from single packaging

London Records
Landmark
Proposal for album boxed set packaging

OPPOSITE
Sarah Brightman
Surrender
Album

Vocals
Guitar / Keyboards
Guitars
Bass
Drums

Nick Holmes
Greg Mackintosh
Aaron Aedy
Stephen Edmondson
Lee Morris

Host

Paradise Lost

Paradise Lost
Images from the Host album sleeve
and the So Much is Lost single

OPPOSITE
Paradise Lost
Icon
Images from packaging for the album
and the EP, Seals the Sense

3:TRUE BELIEF
4:YOUR HAND IN MINE

SWEETNE

Visuals
For every job that goes to print there are always a handful of proposals that end up unused and dispatched to archive oblivion. Here are some that never made it but either stepped aside to make way for a preferred option, or lie in wait hoping to re-appear another day. Included are visuals for: Blur, a well-known lager, Wipeout, Johnny Panic & the Bible of Dreams, Headswim, Squeeze, Reef, Radio 1 Sound City, George Gershwin, Ted Baker, Mansun, Diesel Park West, Listen Up (the lives of Quincy Jones), The Jesus and Mary Chain and Scarlet.

DUMDUMS

DumDums
Can't Get You Out of My Thoughts
Single
OPPOSITE
David Bowie
The Best of, 1969-1974 and 1974-1979
Albums

THE BEST OF DAVID BOWIE 1969/1979

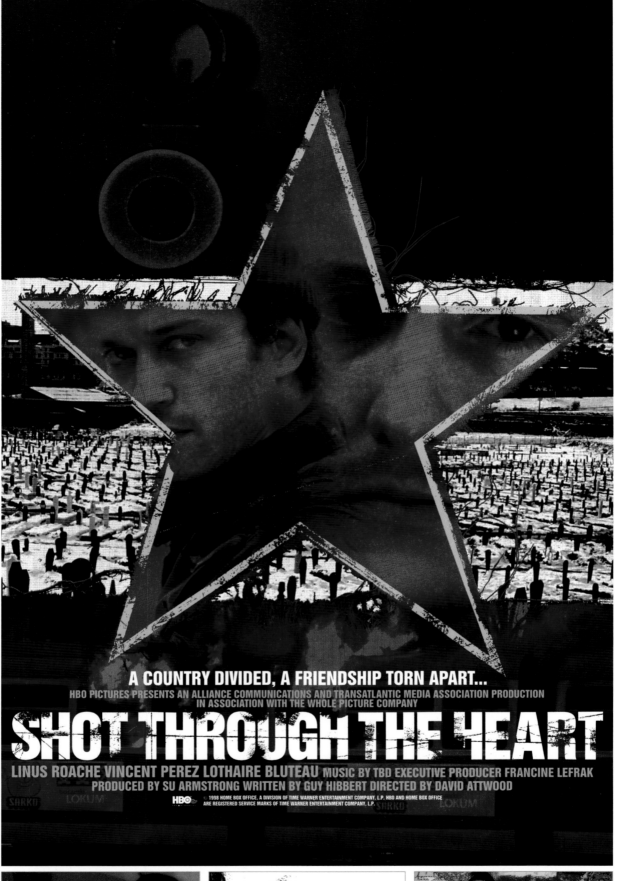

A COUNTRY DIVIDED, A FRIENDSHIP TORN APART...

HBO PICTURES PRESENTS AN ALLIANCE COMMUNICATIONS AND TRANSATLANTIC MEDIA ASSOCIATION PRODUCTION
IN ASSOCIATION WITH THE WHOLE PICTURE COMPANY

SHOT THROUGH THE HEART

LINUS ROACHE VINCENT PEREZ LOTHAIRE BLUTEAU MUSIC BY TBD EXECUTIVE PRODUCER FRANCINE LEFRAK
PRODUCED BY SU ARMSTRONG WRITTEN BY GUY HIBBERT DIRECTED BY DAVID ATTWOOD

HBO 1998 HOME BOX OFFICE, A DIVISION OF TIME WARNER ENTERTAINMENT COMPANY, L.P. HBO AND HOME BOX OFFICE
ARE REGISTERED SERVICE MARKS OF TIME WARNER ENTERTAINMENT COMPANY, L.P.

Kula Shaker
K
Album
OPPOSITE
Shot Through The Heart
Proposal for film poster
Thelonius Monk:
Straight No Chaser
Film poster
Parker
Film poster
Edward II
Proposal for film poster

Superphenix
Images from album packaging

OPPOSITE
Superphenix
Album (front image)

Albert Camus
The Outsider
Book Jacket
OPPOSITE
The Poets
Welcome To The Heathen Reserve
Album and images from packaging
Shooting Star
Single

FFF
Blast Culture
Album

OPPOSITE
Pictor 9
Image for Photolibrary
advertising campaign

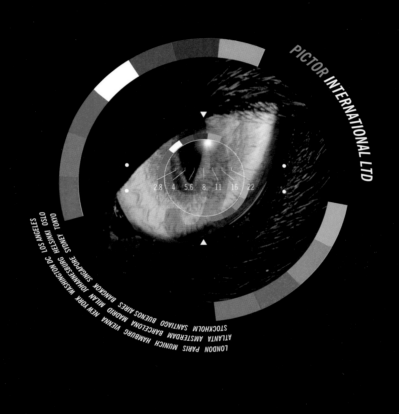

PICTOR INTERNATIONAL LTD

2.8 4 5.6 8 11 16 22

LONDON PARIS MUNICH HAMBURG VIENNA NEW YORK LOS ANGELES
ATLANTA AMSTERDAM BARCELONA MADRID MILAN JOHANNESBURG HELSINKI OSLO
STOCKHOLM SANTIAGO BUENOS AIRES BANGKOK SINGAPORE SYDNEY TOKYO WASHINGTON DC

Simple Minds
Good News From The Next World
Elements from album campaign

During a four year working relationship
with Simple Minds, Good News brought a
new look for the (now two-piece) band.
A photo shoot in the Indian city of Jaipur
produced a wealth of images and a strong
feeling of texture and warm colour.

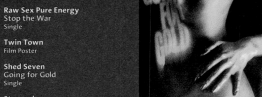

Raw Sex Pure Energy
Stop the War
Single

Twin Town
Film Poster

Shed Seven
Going for Gold
Single

Strangelove
Hysteria Unknown
Single

Octopus
Your Smile
Single

UB40
Kingston Town
Single

Life's Addiction
Jesus Coming In For The Kill
Single

OPPOSITE
The Wall
Dirges and Anthems
Album

THE DIRGES &
WALL ANTHEMS

Stylorouge & Blur A very British coup

by Andrew Collins

You can almost hear the sneer coming through the page whenever Blur are described as an 'art school band'. The connotations of 'art school' or even 'art' within the parameters of the horny-handed world of rock'n'roll is one of pretension, timewasting, even privilege – as if opting for the visual arts at higher education is the exclusive preserve of moneyed fops with no need of a real job at the end of it. (Would that it were in the stiflingly vocational education system of post-Thatcher Britain.)

Art students may have been layabouts with charcoal under their fingertips who fancied themselves a bit, but without them rock music after Elvis would have been poorer indeed: John Lennon, Bryan Ferry, David Bowie, Pete Townshend, Brian Eno, Freddie Mercury, Thom Yorke… even Bauhaus, who actually named themselves after an art school! (Note that this list is all British – The Velvet Underground are probably the closest America's ever come to producing a band with an art school image, thanks to Andy Warhol's patronage, and they weren't really.) So Blur are an art school band. Actually, though Damon Albarn and Alex James both

attended Goldsmiths College, they were studying music and French respectively, and Dave Rowntree did an HND in computer science – but why let the truth get in the way of a good label? Graham Coxon was the real art student, a graduate of both Essex School of Art and Goldsmiths. Blur, or Seymour as they were then, pretty much formed at Goldsmiths, and their first 'proper' gig was at the 1989 degree show – the year Damien Hirst graduated (Sarah Lucas was also in the audience).

It may be opportunistic to describe four people in terms of one collective outlook, but Blur do seem to have an artistic side. While even the scruffiest of bands cares about its image (okay, perhaps not Coldplay), Blur have always taken a healthy interest in the whole package. Which is where Stylorouge come in.

For me, the collaboration between Blur and Stylorouge is unique in rock history – uniquely symbiotic, uniquely long-lasting, and uniquely British. Certainly other bands have enjoyed protracted relationships with one designer or design house – Yes and Roger Dean, New Order and Peter Saville, Pink Floyd and Hipgnosis,

Blur
Starshaped
Image for video packaging

blur

Blur
Popscene
Poster for single

OPPOSITE
Leisure
Album

Boys & Girls
Single

Bang
Single

For Tomorrow
Single

There's No Other Way
Single

Sunday Sunday
Single

Parklife
Album

the Sex Pistols and Jamie Reid, the 4AD roster and Vaughan Oliver – but there is something about the coming-together of Blur and Stylorouge that says something about the cultural and political times in which they worked.

The story of their symbiosis is the story of the Nineties, of a paradigm shift in pop-cultural orthodoxy which took place in this country and categorically not in America, where the MTV Eighties continued to rotate onwards throughout the next decade (Motley Crue turned into Marilyn Manson and nobody noticed).

It is neat that Blur's first single, and by definition Stylorouge's first sleeve for them, should occur in 1990, the first year of a new decade that began, unofficially, with the collapse of the Berlin Wall in 1989. With unification and globalisation came separatism and nationalism, and by the time of the American invasion of 1991 (Nirvana, Seattle and grunge), it was time to repel borders. In 1992

Britpop was born, and the geocultural battle lines were drawn. It was them and us. "Who do you think you are kidding, Mr Cobain?" asked Select magazine in their pivotal Union Jack issue (I should know – I was there, at the heart of bomber command).

By 1992, Blur were old news, history even. After exploding onto a scene of the music papers' making with There's No Other Way and 1991's Leisure album, the commercial spark seemed to have been snuffed out as fast as it had been lit: Popscene went to number 32 and hasty obituaries were written (and a hellish 44-date tour of America almost broke the band's spirit). Thus it was that Blur were not recruited for Select's Britpop home guard - it was all Suede, Pulp, The Auteurs and, somewhat improbably, Denim. (Oasis had yet to record a note.)

But Blur were the very essence of Britpop – if, that is, we define it by a certain aesthetic sophistication and a knowing wink

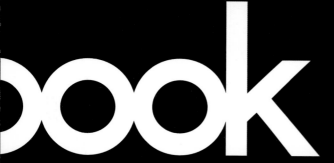

rather than as some Blair-stamped wing of the Department of Trade and Industry. It's there in the band's durable logo – the lower-case understatement combined with the user-friendly curves and the kitsch nod to another age (or at least to another product). The artwork for She's So High had challenged Eighties political correctness with a humorous image by Pop Artist Mel Ramos of a naked girl on a hippopotamus ("It got us into just the right amount of trouble," commented Food Records boss Dave Balfe). Though the laddish revisionism of Loaded and FHM would soon come to characterise the Nineties, Blur and Stylorouge got in early; polytechnic feminists were inspired to reflect loudly upon the nature of art and pornography – and Blur grabbed some column inches in the news pages. They put a couple of cocks on the sleeve of Bang, perhaps just to redress the balance.

Blur and their artwork were not designed to shock, rather to stimulate. Access to 'style books' prepared for the band by Stylorouge and to the reams of unused sleeve designs is illuminating indeed to those who see a marriage made in media heaven. For Popscene, for instance, we see a cut-out of the Queen Mother against some floral wallpaper (in the end, they plumped for a dog carrying a pheasant). Girls And Boys – which ended up like a packet of condoms – might have been an Alsatian sniffing a poodle's bum. Parklife might have been a male model in tennis gear from some godforsaken catalogue, or the grille of a Rolls Royce, or an over-the-top royal coat of arms that echoes an early Queen album. So many images, so many cultural touchstones, so little time!

The apparently insatiable appetite for misappropriating found images was like a furnace into which Stylorouge shovelled endless coal. No kitsch possibility was left untapped, from teenage boy's birthday card and Ralph Lauren polo shirt to beer mat and collectible china plate.

It is no coincidence that the 'British Image' photographs marked the critical turning point for Blur around the time of Modern Life Is Rubbish in 1993. The audacity of naming one of your own press

blurb

Blur
The Great Escape
Images for the inside and back of the
album packaging

OPPOSITE
Great Escape
Street poster for the release of the single

shots – 'British Image 1' (Fred Perrys, Doc Martens and Great Dane) – highlights Blur's arch understanding of self-packaging. Modern Life Is Rubbish was not just a title taken from some graffiti in the Bayswater Road, it was a profound statement on the condition of Britain. The old-fashioned painting of a train harked back to some bygone, steam-driven age, when life apparently wasn't rubbish.

By the time of the artificially stoked Blur-Oasis wars of 1995, the upbeat oompah and Benny Hill video of Country House masked strained relations within the band. It was Graham – bloody art student! – who most resented the seemingly laddish new direction and the pop-star trappings (and he who winced the hardest at the din of screaming girls). But the sleeves from the Great Escape period reflect a world-beating swagger: the pin-sharp parodies of Disneyland ('Blur World'), Microsoft (back of The Great Escape) and even Alien (The Universal). In truth, like Blur's mainstream pop success, the band's visual identity

would soon be due for a change of direction. It had been an incredible three-album journey.

The band retreated (Damon to Iceland, Alex to Soho, Dave to the skies and Graham into his US noise records) and when they returned, with the regenerative, reductive Blur album, it came wrapped in enigmatic artwork by Chris Thompson (now flown from Stylorouge to his new company Yacht Associates). The outlook had changed: no more visual gags, no more artistic sampling, no more CD-sized critiques of Britain – in their place, well, a blur. By the time of Tender and the 13 album in 1997, Graham's fine art had symbolically emerged as the new corporate image of Blur (just as his musical belligerence now drove their sound).

By now, Britpop as a notion was past its sell-by date. To prove its naffness, it was appropriated by the new government and resold as 'Cool Britannia', a concept dreamt up by a New Labour think tank. The minute Noel Gallagher stepped into Number 10 for canapes,

the dream – as Lennon had declared on the song God – was over. It is hard to credit it now, but there was a time when the tag Britpop was not an embarrassment. Between 1990 and 1997, British music staked its most convincing claim on the rest of the world since Beatlemania, Elton John and Duran Duran. (Wouldn't you know it – Blur only really caught on in America with Song 2, a throwaway blast from their fuck-off Blur album.)

The legacy of Blur's relationship with Stylorouge is there for all to see: in the smartest visual CV of any band since glory-years Pink Floyd. Yet while the Floyd and Hipgnosis truly created their own universe with sleeves like Wish You Were Here and Animals, Blur and Stylorouge reflected the real world. You can read Blur's sleeves like a biography of a decade – the Nineties are much harder to thumbnail than, say, the Sixties (swinging) or the Eighties (greed), but through Blur's jackdaw plunder of British imagery they said a lot about the state of the nation at the end of a century.

The Nineties were a time of deconstruction and reconstruction, patriotism (Euro 96, "Up Yours, Delors!") and regeneration (new lads, New Labour, the new rock'n'roll).

Blur stood at the middle of all that made the decade interesting. Stylorouge found a willing and proactive conduit for their endless love of printed material and easy knack for lateral thinking (Parklife – greyhounds; Chemical World – Athena).
It is apt that they were responsible for visualising that other key Nineties talisman, Trainspotting, a film that managed to embody British export optimism despite being shot through with smack and a scabrous disregard for national pride ("I hate being Scottish. The English are just wankers. We on the other hand are colonised by wankers").

Likewise, Britain backed Blur – and Blur took the piss out of Britain. They truly were were a kick up the Nineties. And I'm happy to say that both band and design company are still going strong. Not bad for a bunch of bloody art students.

blur The Great Escape

Blur
The Great Escape
Image for front of the album

Blur
Boys And Girls
Single Visual (with
accompanying notes written
by Dave Balfe of Food Records)

OPPOSITE
Dr John
Anutha Zone
Album

Designed for extra
sensation.

DR JOHN

ANUTHA ZONE

Yura
Beyond The Pale
Album

Headswim
Despite Yourself/
Tourniquet
Elements From Album/
Single Packaging

HEADSWIM

despite yourself

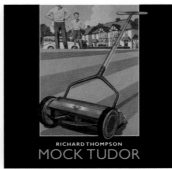

Paddy Casey
Amen (So Be It)
Proposal for album

Richard Thompson
Mock Tudor
Album

Kula Shaker
Tattva
Single

Shack
HMS Fable
Album

OPPOSITE
Joan Armatrading
Hearts and Flowers
Album

Fashion Forum
2 exciting programmes of
seminars and presentations
arranged by Banks Sadler
in the fashion capitals
of Europe.

Redtape
Music from the
Third Floor
CBS promotional cassette

OPPOSITE
Fashion Forums
Poster image

1

2

3

4

7

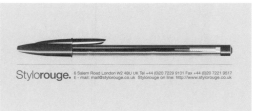

9

5

6

8

#2 Stylorouge: Carton
(123mm x 54mm) Ink on cotton

10

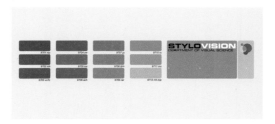

11

12

13

14

15

16

17

18

19

20

21

22

23

24

25

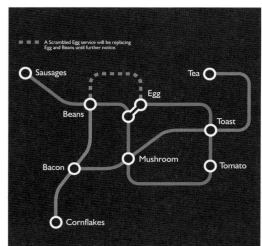

26

27

28

29

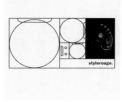

1

2

3

4

5

6

7

Apparel

8

9

10

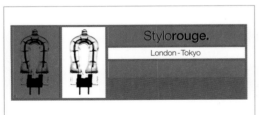

11

12

13

14

15

16

Danielle Dax
Blast the Human Flower
Album (front)
OPPOSITE
Danielle Dax
Blast the Human Flower
Album (back)

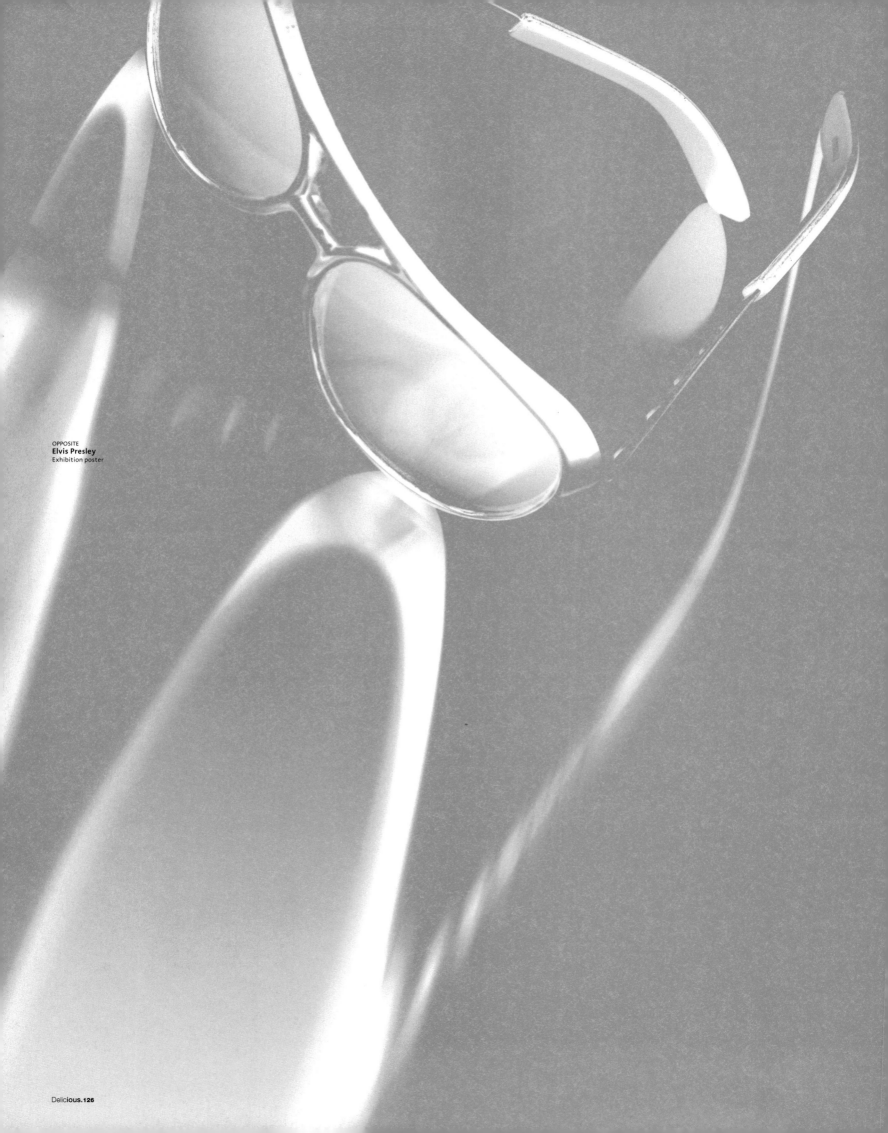

OPPOSITE
Elvis Presley
Exhibition poster

ELVIS

ELVIS PRESLEY THE EXHIBITION

Kinky Machine.

#5.1993."Kinky Machine". Gouache & Ink on livestock. Private collection.

THE NEXT BIG THING

2 RUN ON EMPTY

3 LOOK OUT

1 TOMORROW

4 top OF

THE WORLD

5 RAILS

7 CHEMIC- AL #1

6 WISHING IT AWAY

8 MOTION

9 THEY'RE OUT THERE

10 FOR A MOMENT

11 ADDICTION

OBSESSION 8 ME 12 FEBRUARY

LOON ON THE

GETHER

JESUS JONES ALREADY

SIOUXSIE AND THE BANSHEES
ONCE UPON A TIME
THE SINGLES

INCLUDING HONG KONG GARDEN/MIRAGE
THE STAIRCASE (MYSTERY) PLAYGROUND TWIST
LOVE IN A VOID/HAPPY HOUSE/CHRISTINE/ISRAEL
SPELLBOUND/ARABIAN KNIGHTS

Jesus Jones
Various clockwise from top:

Oops
Page from Stylorouge book
Celebration featuring the album
sleeve of Liquidizer

Doubt
Album

Info Freako
Single

Perverse
Proposal for special album packaging

Info Psycho
Single

OPPOSITE
Jesus Jones
Photograph of singer Mike Edwards

Ooops. The number of TV channels available to the British people has just doubled. Thanks to Mr. Murdoch and his Sky TV satellite, £5 million well spent, mate. Author Salman Rushie is not bothered anyway - he's suddenly found his spare time sitting around the house double top. The Satanic Verses: "All those involved in its publication who were aware of its content are sentenced to death." - now that's what I call a bad review. Mrs. Bhutto's a granny, official! The ozone layer's got a hole in the ozone. The captain of US oil tanker Exxon Valdez is pissed, it's heading for a reef off the coast of Alsaka! Oooops. Topical mid-1989 joke: What do you do if a rottweiler starts making love to your leg? Fake an orgasm. Advertising hoardings across the South East ask, "HLF, can anyone make sense of it?" The total number of people who have contracted botulism from hazelnut yogurt rises to 22 in June. One in three people in Glasgow have not paid their Poll Tax. Oooops. One wall without accompanying satellite dish comes down in Berlin. Pssst! Wanna buy some water? "Is it IFLE Bob?"

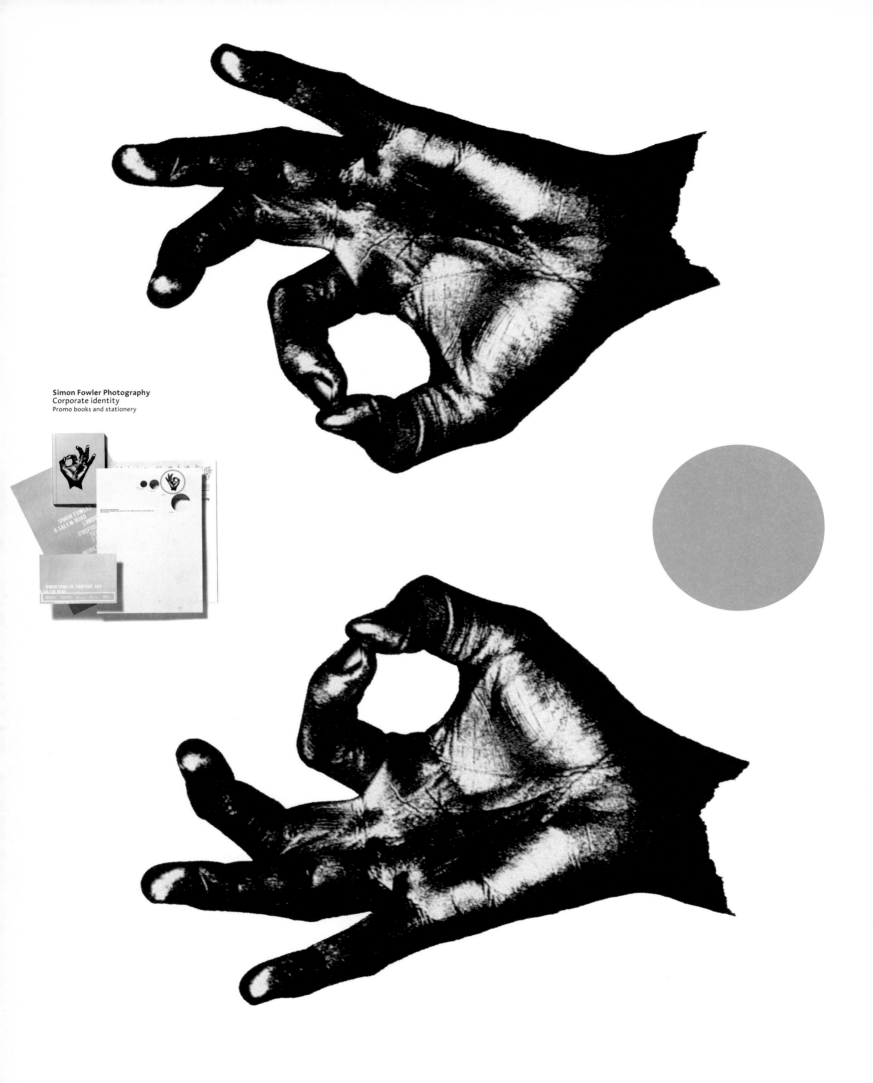

Simon Fowler Photography
Corporate identity
Promo books and stationery

Prima Diva

Beethoven
Symphonien
56
WOLFGANG SAWALLISCH

TCHAIKOVSKY
Passion

WORLD PREMIERE OF DAVID BINTLEY'S
FULL LENGTH BALLET FOR THE COMPANY
Cyrano.
A LAVISH
17th CENTURY
ROMANTIC
ADVENTURE

MUSIC WILFRED JOSEPHS   CHOREOGRAPHER DAVID BINTLEY
DESIGNER HAYDEN GRIFFIN   LIGHTING JOHN B. READ

SPONSORED (1991) BY THE JEAN SAINSBURY ROYAL OPERA HOUSE FUND
AND THE LINBURY TRUST

BOX OFFICE
071 240 1066/1911

2,4,6*,8*,15,23,27,29 MAY
1 JUNE AT 7.30 PM
*MIDLAND BANK PROMS

ROYAL
OPERA
HOUSE
Covent Garden

Prima Diva
Compilation album

Cyrano
Poster

Schumann/Schnittke
Cello Concertos
Album

Beethoven
Symphonien 56
Album

Tchaikovsky
Passion
Proposal for album

Tchaikovsky
The Dance Album

Emmanuel Pahud
Flute Concertos
Album

Roger Norrington
Mozart Requiem
Album

Tchaikovsky
THE DANCE ALBUM

EMMANUEL
PAHUD
HAYDN-ENSEMBLE BERLIN
HANSJÖRG SCHELLENBERGER

ROGER NORRINGTON
MOZART
REQUIEM
MAURERISCHE TRAUERMUSIK / AVE VERUM CORPUS

Kula Shaker
Peasants, Pigs & Astronauts
Images from the campaigns for the album and the singles, Mystical Machine Gun and Shower Your Love

Strangelove
Visionary
EP

Echo and the Bunnymen
Rust
Single

Propellerheads
On Her Majesty's Secret Service
Single

Momo
Arabesque
Album

OPPOSITE
Pink Floyd
Dark Side of the Moon
Elements for 20th anniversary release of
the album (with Storm Thorgesen)

Pink Floyd Dark Side Of The Moon
Twentieth Anniversary Edition

Crowded House
Recurring Dream
Images from the Best Of campaign:
Shots from the location hunt in
New Zealand
One of the resulting promotional
shots of the band
Polaroids taken during the shoot at
the house of a friend of the band

OPPOSITE

Graphics used throughout
the campaign
Packaging and point-of-sale for
the single Instinct

Crowded House had always
arranged their own album artwork,
and Recurring Dream, the Best Of
album, was no exception. Bass
player Nick Seymour had already
painted an enigmatic piece for the
album front by the time
Stylorouge had been approached.
Our brief was to put the artwork
together with Nick and work with
photographer Andy Earl to produce
a range of band shots which could
be used for press, packaging, and
the marketing campaign.
Rob O'Connor and Andy travelled
to New Zealand for a week. Several
locations were found and used
during the three days of the shoot,
including the recording studio,
a ramshackle wooden cottage,
a house in the hilly suburbs of
Auckland and the rugged coastline
where the main picture here was
taken. We painted the boat red
(with the owner's permission of
course), to add colour.
On their return to London a
meagre half hours worth of Super
Eight footage, shot by O'Connor
during the three days, was cut to
create the promo video for the
single Everything Is Good For You.
When the album was due for
release the band announced their
decision to split. We don't think
our involvement had any bearing
on this development.

Come **Together**

by Rob O'Connor

I'm one of those people who stay glued to my seat at the end of a movie when the credits roll. I'm not sure why – there's hardly any chance I'm going to recognise the name of the best boy or the location caterers, although I do like to check out the more obscure tracks that get thrown into the aural jumble sale that constitutes the modern soundtrack.

What transfixes me is the sheer quantity of names – all those people doing what they do best for a common aim – make up artists, set builders, costume designers... credits where they're due. A feature film may or may not encapsulate the vision of one man or woman, but each contributing talent will inevitably help create its look and feel, from the starring actors through to the electricians. It is this embodiment of the team ethic that I find so fascinating.

When I accepted the invitation to co-direct the promotional video for Maxi Priest's *Some Guys Have All The Luck* many years ago, I experienced my first taste of film-making (well alright, video). It was such a buzz then – as it is now, but not so far removed from the process of producing still pictures, which until then had been as far as my direction career had gone. In the stills business, though, it is more common to assume the title of art director.

This job title causes so much confusion to graphic design students and tutors alike. The whole concept of evaluating individual ability is put in jeopardy when someone's overwhelming talent is for communicating their ideas to others and guiding them while they do the actual work (a photographer, for example). In my opinion the collaboration of people with varied skills isn't just an interesting way to realise a creative vision, it is fundamental to the way we work at Stylorouge. While remaining fervently protective of our individual ideas, we indulge and encourage each other. If 'brainstorming' isn't too pretentious or naff an expression then, well, that's what we do. We each have particular strengths. Some of us work in a more illustrative way, some of us are more technically minded or photographically biased, confident with colour, accomplished with type. It allows us more breadth and scope, and helps keep us open minded about creative possibilities.

The other aspect of this team ethic is probably an obvious one – that is of utilising the talents of people outside Stylorouge – in other words, photographers and illustrators. However much we enjoy taking our own pictures and, on occasion, creating the odd illustration, we doff our caps to the better-qualified practitioners on a regular basis. I am grateful that we have been able to work with some great people in both areas and will continue to learn from the experience of setting up photo shoots with Simon Fowler, Andy Earl, Nick Knight, Sheila Rock, David Scheinmann and so on.

In our nursery years, such collaborations had to be negotiated carefully as budgets were generally low. But the reward was the prospect of greater creative freedom.

Photographers often offered their talent in return for a portfolio-bound job and a 50/50 split of the modest spoils (net, of course). In this way, fulfilling and enjoyable jobs were completed for some of our favourite projects – The Passions, Shriekback, Music For Pleasure. A spirit of collaboration was born.

Like many who had studied the relatively new subject of graphic design, art direction had been an enigma to me, at best something that had probably evolved during the Fifties, in the heyday of American advertising where images of utopian everyday life were created to sell everything from cars to cornflakes (automobiles to Cheerios to you). The Rockwellian visions of middle-class America had created the template for their photographic successors.

In the British underground of the 1970s, Hipgnosis kidnapped the art of the visual narrative through their contrivance of photographic reality and made it their own, with Storm Thorgesen and his partners employing the best pre-press craftsmen in the advertising industry to achieve optimum visual realism. (These were the pre-computer Seventies). In New York, ex-pat Parisien Jean-Paul Goude plied his trade at *Esquire* under the guidance of his magazine design guru George Lois. Fired-up by the manipulative potential of the creative photograph he became Grace Jones' art director, svengali and sometime partner and utilised her striking appearance to make some of the most exciting and remarkable record covers, videos and live performances of the early Eighties. As art directors both Goude and Thorgesen have influenced me, and I have also since had the pleasure of working with them. My own approach to art direction is less theatrical, erring on the side of subtlety. I am intrigued by visuals that work on a more subliminal level.

When we launched our first web site in 1996, we included a company manifesto. Our attitude towards collaboration as part of the creative process was referred to in the closing paragraph. We haven't changed our outlook much and long may we stand by our philosophy:

"We try to balance the analytical approach to visual 'problem solving', (some folk refer to this as having ideas), with a forward-looking intuitive flair (except on Monday mornings). Working collaboratively is enjoyed and encouraged; we treasure our associations with such talented practitioners as photographers and illustrators and value these experiences as an educational continuation. We hold all kinds of creativity in high esteem. Dignity and justice dictate that nothing is done for nothing and in our experience optimum success and quality result from the most respectful relationships. Nothing puts a bigger smile on our faces than driving a job from bottom to top: Concept, Art Direction, Design, Typography, Artwork, Repro, Pub; and in that order. We will turn our hands to most things and hopefully enter creative dialogue with a receptive ear and practical demeanour."

Straw
Sailing off the Edge of The World
Proposal for single

OPPOSITE
Blur
Modern Life is Rubbish
Album

Pop music is not complicated...

THE BLUE OX BABES
APPLES AND ORANGES
(THE INTERNATIONAL HOPE CAMPAIGN)

helicopter girl
345 wonderful →

Helicopter Girl
345 Wonderful
Proposal for single
OPPOSITE
Blue Ox Babes
Apples and Oranges
Single

SUBCIRCUS/ 60 SECOND LOVE AFFAIR/
...ENCE HAS A SOUND/ DON'T YOU
...EAR... IN A MAGICAL PUFF OF SMOKE/
...S LIKE WE JUST MIGHT MAKE IT THROUGH/
...IXTY SECONDS/ IT LOOKS LIKE WE HAVE
...METHING SO NEW/ AND IT WILL PROTECT
...ALLING/

S7846
22kV

'94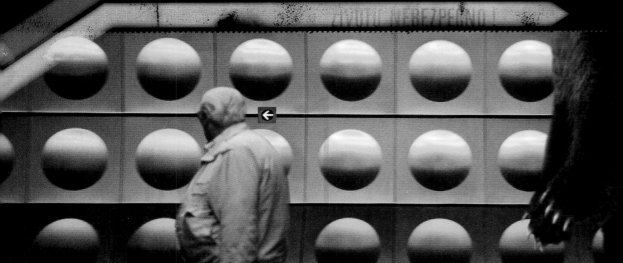

Václavské   Můstek   náměstí

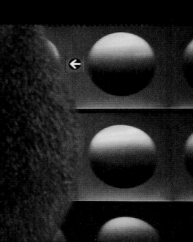

**Dave Stewart and
Barbara Gaskin**
The Big Idea
Album

OPPOSITE

All About Eve
What Kind Of Fool
Single

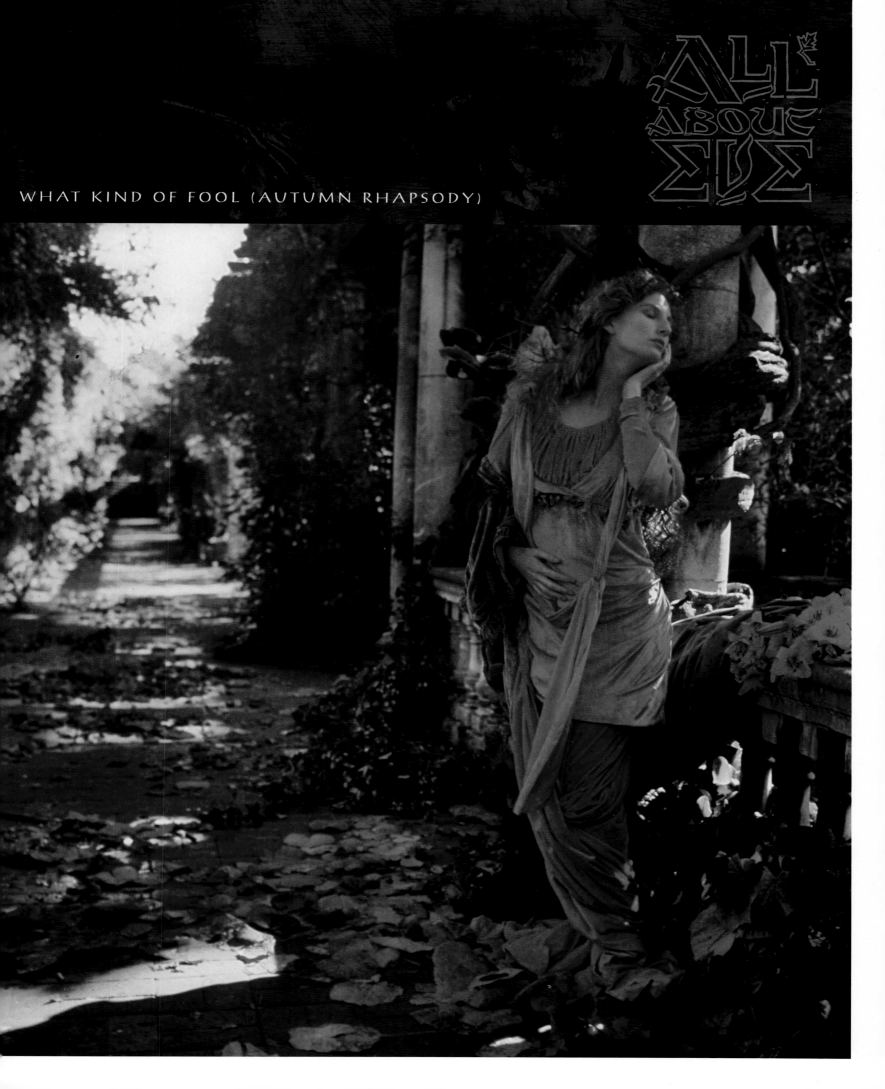

All About Eve
Various Images

Stylorouge produced a number of
designs for All About Eve over
several years, many of which were
only seen by die-hard fans, which
is often the case.
The selection here are from
various album and single
campaigns including Scarlet and
Other Stories, Touched by Jesus
and What kind of Fool

'Farewell Mr.Sorrow'
ALL ABOUT EVE

'The Dreamer'
ALL ABOUT EVE

ALL ABOUT EVE
'Strange Way'

FEBRUARY, 1949

ALL ABOUT EVE

Rolling Stones
No Security
Full page press ad

OPPOSITE
Rolling Stones
No Security
Album

An attempt to identify the contents of the album without relying on mere words... No Security is the most recent in a careers worth of live Rolling Stones albums. We travelled to some of the band's European stadium concerts with photographer Zed Nelson and photographed people in pairs who had arrived early for the show. The two on the right (at the Vienna show) were favoured over a motley bunch.
The picture presented us with the possible title Security (the Stones added the word No).

Within the ad image:

ROLLING STONES NO SECURITY.
LIVE FROM THE BRIDGES TO BABYLON TOUR
CD/MC/LP/MINI DISC. OUT 2.11
YOU GOT ME ROCKING GIMME SHELTER FLIP THE SWITCH MEMORY MOTEL CORINNA SAINT OF ME
WAITING ON A FRIEND SISTER MORPHINE LIVE WITH ME RESPECTABLE THIEF IN THE NIGHT
THE LAST TIME OUT OF CONTROL

Virgin "ROLLING STONES" and Tongue and Lip Design are Trademarks of Musidor B.V. Printed in the USA.

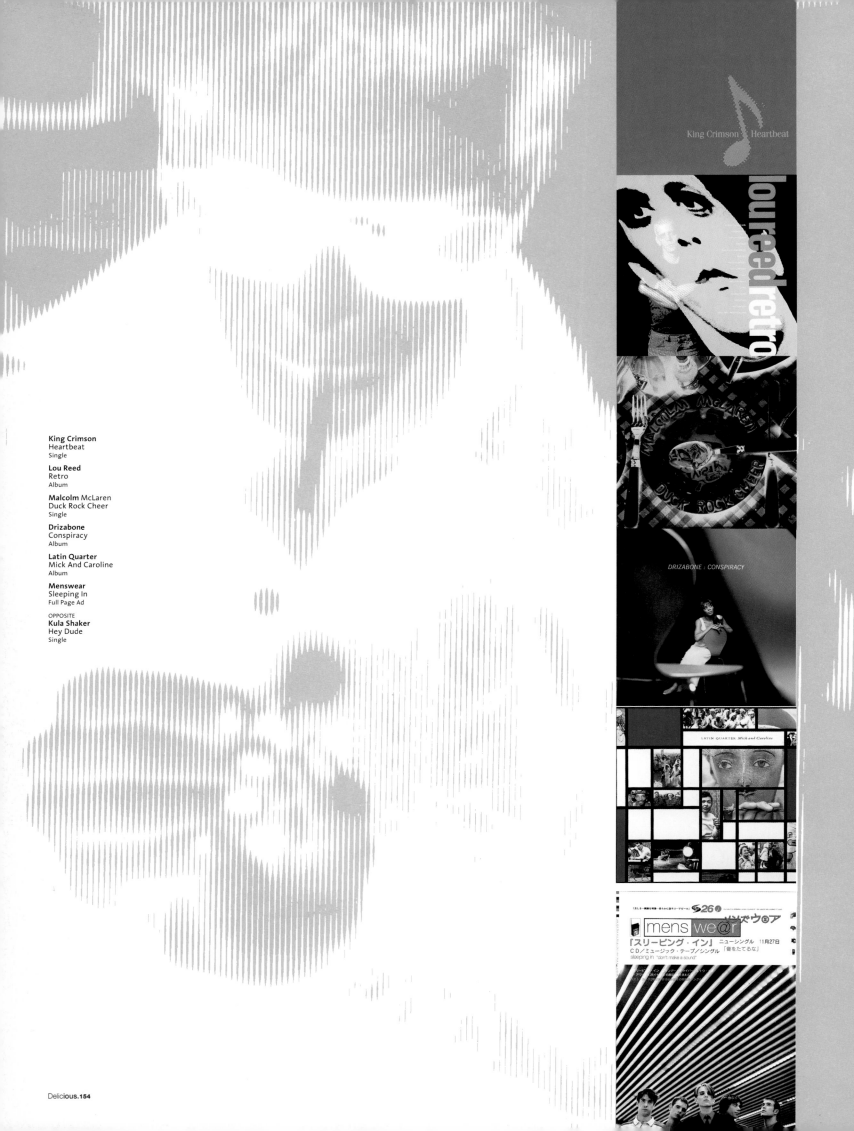

King Crimson
Heartbeat
Single

Lou Reed
Retro
Album

Malcolm McLaren
Duck Rock Cheer
Single

Drizabone
Conspiracy
Album

Latin Quarter
Mick And Caroline
Album

Menswear
Sleeping In
Full Page Ad

OPPOSITE
Kula Shaker
Hey Dude
Single

Pooka
City Sick (EP)
EP

Baby Chaos
Hello Victim
Single (front)

Alexei Sayle
Albanian! Albania!
Single

Straw
Keepsakes
Album Cover

Baby Chaos
Hello Victim
Single (back)

Blancmange
I Can See It
Single

OPPOSITE
Echobelly
On
Album Inner Spreads

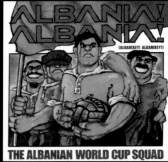

the new album, cassette and c.d. includes the singles "hourglass" and "trust me to open my mouth"

squeeze

babylon and on

squeeze u.k. tour and on and on – thursday 17th sept. – london astoria / friday 18th sept. – aylesbury civic hall / saturday 19th sept. – leicester de montfort hall / sunday 20th sept. – manchester apollo / tuesday 22nd sept. – birmingham powerhouse / wednesday 23rd sept. – notts royal concert hall / thursday 24th sept. – oxford apollo / saturday 26th. sept. – liverpool royal court theatre / sunday 27th sept. – glasgow pavilion / monday 28th sept. – edinburgh queens theatre / wednesday 30th sept. – hammersmith odeon / thursday 1st oct.– poole arts centre / friday 2nd oct. – cardiff university / friday 9th oct. – norwich university of east anglia / saturday 10th oct. – loughborough university / sunday 11th oct. – bristol studio / monday 12th oct. – brighton top rank / tuesday 13th oct. – folkestone leas cliff hall / friday 16th oct. – leeds university / saturday 17th oct. – sheffield university / monday 19th oct. – guildford civic hall / tuesday 20th oct. – cheltenham town hall / thursday 22nd oct. – portsmouth guild hall / saturday 24th oct. – hanley victoria hall / sunday 25th oct. – newcastle mayfair

8535937

Squeeze
From top:

Hourglass
Single

8535937
Single

The Waiting Game
Single

Footprints
Single

Some Fantastic Place
Image from single

OPPOSITE
Squeeze
Babylon and on
Album tour poster

TED BAKER WORLD LEADERS

Prφmφtіл9 ρедсе тнгφцɥн Style

TED BAKER

TED BAKER
LONDON

Ted Baker
World Leaders
One of a series of In-store posters

World Leaders
Condom packet

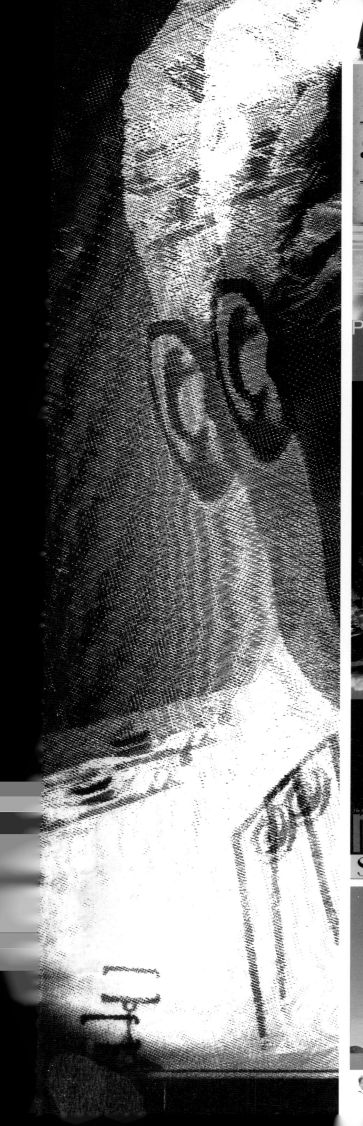

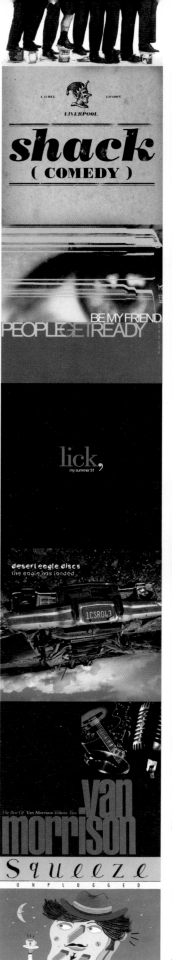

Chris
Sheehan
Out Of The
Woods.

Chris Sheehan
Out Of The Woods
Album

OPPOSITE
**Buddy Curtess And The
Grasshoppers**
Photo from gig poster

Shack
Comedy
Single

People Get Ready
Be My Friend
Single

Lick
My Summer '57
Single

Desert Eagle Discs
The Eagle Has Landed
Album

Van Morrison
Best Of Volume 2
Album

Squeeze
Unplugged
Cover of Unplugged tour Brochure

**Buddy Curtess And The
Grasshoppers**
Photo from gig poster (second half)

T+CP

Echo and the Bunnymen, The Teardrop Explodes, The Pale Fountains, Bradford Park Avenue, The Wheeltappers and Shunters Social Club, Town & Country Planning – they kind of roll off the tongue don't they? They're not entirely unrelated, the common bond being the north of England. When Martyn Atkins came south in 1980, it was to put his design skills to work, briefly as the first of many hard-working aides of Peter Saville, and then in his own right under the tongue-in-cheek name Town & Country Planning. By the time the name was familiar in the music industry and was generally abbreviated to T&CP, the personnel had increased to three. All of them inspired by art, music and football they also all hailed from West Yorkshire, but somehow here they were breathing the same London air, first in an underground concrete bunker in Lancaster Gate then in a maisonette-cum-studio in Notting Hill. In a short time, they were responsible for some of the most memorable music design to come out of Britain in the Eighties.

Packaging for the aforementioned Bunnymen, Teardrop Explodes, and a close relationship with Depeche Mode resulted in award-winning album sleeves, fast-selling merchandise and atmospherically shot videos. But this is another story (perhaps even another book?!). My interest in T&CP beyond friendship and the constant unrealized threat of five-a-side football increased when Martyn decided on a major life change, opting to concentrate on video and film direction in Los Angeles. This would leave Mark and Dave, a West 11 studio, and an enviable reputation in his wake. And that's where Stylorouge came in. We effectively took over the running of T&CP in 1990, retaining its existing client base and utilising the unique personality of its visual output to build new relationships with new companies as diverse as Slow River, Rykodisc, Almo Sounds, deConstruction and Manga. T&CP is currently an army of one, Mark being the sole survivor, whilst continuing to be a full-time collaborative member of the Stylorouge team.

T&CP is now more of a low-key subsidiary, concentrating on artists on the commercial fringes such as Peter Bruntnell and Paul Brady. It remains a sleeping giant ready to be re-awakened for the next golden age.

Cud
Once Again
Single

OPPOSITE
The Balanescu Quartet
Possessed
Album

Almo Sounds
Label Sampler
Album

OPPOSITE
Sleeper
Smart
Album

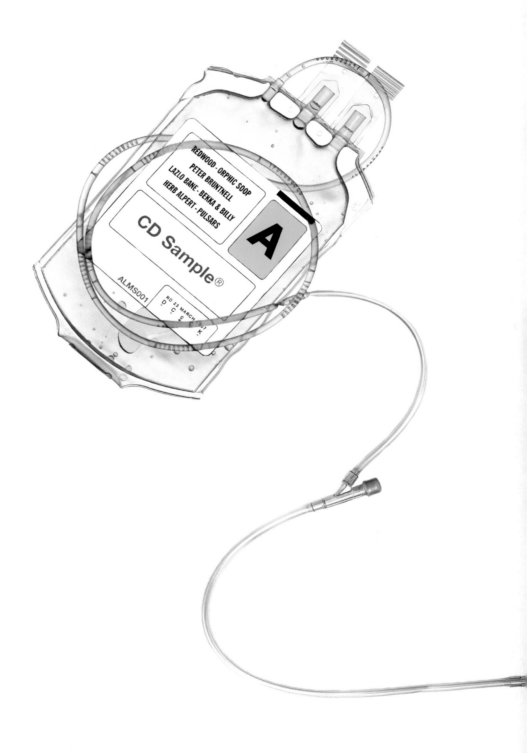

(sleeper)

SMART

red**wood**
FALLING DOWN

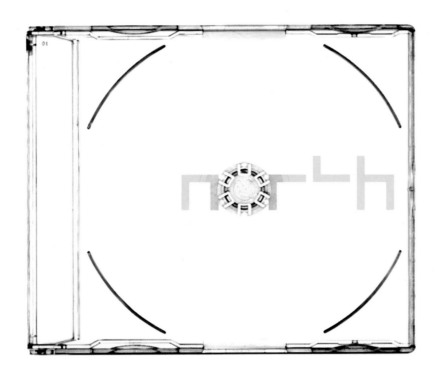

T+CP

Sixty Degrees North
60°N
Range bag/corporate identity

OPPOSITE
Redwood
Falling Down
Single concept

PARDON ME, OH PARDON
FATHOM ME 2 3
_APPLE TREES AT TH
CHARTREUSE ITHINKILOVE–
FATHOM ME EVERY–PE

pardon me.

  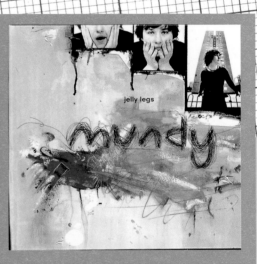

Native Voices
Compilation
Album

OPPOSITE
Hipkiss
Bluebird
Album

Siva Pacifica

Noa

Madredeus

Vision II

Ravi Shankar

Paul Mounsey

Robbie Robertson

Máire Brennan

Jon Anderson

Elbosco

HIPKISS BLUEBIRD

LOVE YOU'RE IN · **AFTER HOURS** · WHERE WE'RE M... ...BIRD · **TURNED** ON
DARK WORLD · **BARBARELLA DISC...** ...RAW LOV... ...OU BELIEVE
DEALS · LATE NIGHT STORY · CARDIGAN LA...

MAIN PICTURE
Love And Money
Strange Kind of Love
Album

An intriguing tableau shot
in a studio-built set,
featuring the band and
various anonymous extras

Above
Jocelyn Square
Press ad for single

Hallelujah Man
Single

Strange Kind of Love
Still-life shot from album sleeve

LOVE *and* MONEY STRANGE *kind of* LOVE

MAIN PICTURE
Squeeze
King George Street
Single

Never shy of wordplay, the band's
choice of Cosi Fan Tutti Frutti as an
album title led to this visual marriage of
opera and rock and roll. One of several
unchosen images originally created for
the album, it was dusted off and
adapted as a single cover when King
George Street was released.

tears for fears the seeds of love

Tears For Fears
The Seeds of Love
Album

Woman in Chains
Single

OPPOSITE
Trainspotting
Renton teaser
Poster

Trainspotting

by Claire Allfree

Think of the film Trainspotting and the chances are you won't think first of a scene from the film, but of its advertising. Gritty black-and-white photographs of five key actors from the film boxed on clean white backgrounds, numbered and captioned with their character names in orange. For years after the film was released, you couldn't escape the look that the campaign defined: everyone from clothing and computer companies to clubs appropriated the image and used it to advertise their own products, all wanting to associate themselves with the film's iconic status, all hoping that a bit of its critical, commercial and cult success would rub off on them. Five years on, Odeon cinemas were still using the design on their customised packets of jelly babies, and some students still have fading reproductions of the original on their walls.

Somehow a film about heroin addiction has become not only one of the best marketed films in living memory but has provided the 20th century with one of its most enduring cultural images.

When Stylorouge first accepted the brief there was some nervousness about the potentially controversial nature of the film, but it being a Danny Boyle project, the buzz was already enormous. Like most people who read Irvine Welsh's original ground breaking book, Stylorouge's Rob O'Connor and Mark Blamire laughed aloud while finding much of it monumentally distasteful. As is typical of Stylorouge's approach to campaign development, everyone on the team discussed ideas for the poster in initial brainstorming meetings, although the number of people who went on to work on the project was limited for practical reasons. The project became O'Connor and Blamire's baby.

Keen to tap into the disenfranchised tone of the book, they first imagined a poster that would convey a grubby sense of danger, as though one would catch something if one went near it. Other early ideas included a re-creation of the scene where Renton plunges into the toilet, dismissed because the ensuing watery image would be too abstract. Also ruled out was PolyGram's idea of having the characters photographed full length and almost in silhouette, standing on a bridge against an urban background, redolent of the promotional shots for Iain Softley's Beatles/Stuart Sutcliffe biopic Backbeat. (PolyGram had originally envisaged the film as a gang/buddy movie, with the cast having a similar no-hoper image to that of a neo-punk band). Indeed it was probably Stylorouge's history of working with bands that brought the project their way. O'Connor and Blamire rejected the idea of urban dislocation however: dirty realism had been done to death in the Sixties; they also wanted to avoid glamourising drugs with heroin-chic imagery.

Instead, they became increasingly interested in branding the characters according to their personality. They were keen to highlight the sense of multiple identity; of the many voices that speak in Irvine Welsh's novel. They also liked the arbitrary nature of the film's title and Blamire started playing with the iconography of train timetables and signage. The idea of taking individual shots of the characters instead of a group began to take precedence – group shots seemed too generic and band-like. At first the team considered deliberately amateurish snaps and photobooth shots, and of using train windows as frames for the individual portraits. They were convinced that the photographs should be black and white, which in itself was a radical proposition; as a rule marketing doesn't aim to undersell the product (Trainspotting is a colour movie of course), and yet O'Connor and Blamire felt that black and white on a clean white background would both de-glamourize the subject and give it a clinical impact. Pharmaceutical packaging also came to mind – hence the boxed information typography and the warning colour orange. Gradually, the poster was taking shape.

Photographer Lorenzo Agius was booked to take test

THIS FILM IS EXPECTED TO ARRIVE...

23:02:96

From the team that brought you Shallow Grave

#1 RENTON

#2 BEGBIE

#3

#4 SICK BOY

#5 SPUD

"Stylorouge's design concept for Trainspotting spawned a legion of imitators and is now a collector's item. The campaign for Trainspotting has gone down in marketing history as a piece of design magic" Screen International

shots of various members of Stylorouge staff to get some idea of both how the cast should be photographed and how the panels and numbering devices could be incorporated. These shots received the green light from PolyGram and producer, Andrew MacDonald, and a date for the proper photo shoot was set.

When it came to the day of the photo shoot, the cast were exhausted and emotionally ill-prepared; the poster campaign was so ahead of schedule that the film itself was not yet in post-production; in fact the 'wrap' party had taken place only the night before and the last scene had been shot that very morning. The aesthetic demands of the film had taken their toll; they were skinny, rundown and in emotional turmoil. Ewan McGregor resigned himself to being photographed soaking wet. Jonny Lee Miller was less happy to assume a James Bond pose, but the experienced professional Robert Carlyle pulled him round. Perhaps Lee Miller should be grateful; Kevin McKidd, who played Tommy in the film and who was not at the shoot, didn't make it onto the poster at all, and as a consequence is arguably less of a 'household face' than his colleagues. During the shoot, the precaution was taken of shooting group photographs as well as individuals, but when it came to it, the individuals were considerably more powerful. The resulting black-and-white images were presented to PolyGram and Macdonald who both loved them.

With the start of the student year fast approaching,

Stylorouge designed a teaser campaign, as well as producing an ad campaign for the daily published Cannes Festival Magazine, distributed by Screen International. And thus, with the campaign so well prepared, a buzz was already growing, way ahead of the film's release date.

The finished poster needs little description – it is burnt into the retina of public consciousness, and its iconic status has been officially acknowledged: the poster was recognized by D&AD (Design & Art Direction) and the campaign went on to win various categories at the Screen International awards. Despite its visual simplicity and immediacy, its core strength lies in its powerful ambiguity. The first phase of the campaign was a series of solo character posters; the first 'group' poster had the actors isolated in boxes. The black-and-white definition has a sophistication redolent of a fashion shoot yet looking at these images is disorientating; the characters seem larger than life, they rear up at you in slightly monstrous fashion. The lack of romance and cosmetic deception looks disarmingly unlike a film poster but feels faithful to the film.

If Trainspotting the film redefined British cinema then Trainspotting the poster redefined the way it was marketed. Most of all it captured a butterfly-from-the-chrysalis moment when British marketing culture suddenly found a new identity; one of arrogant independence, confident of its product and most of all, having the balls to take risks.

Trainspotting
Poster

OPPOSITE (LEFT TO RIGHT)
A handful of the thousands of look-a-like campaigns

Poster visuals prepared using the test photo session and oth initial proposals

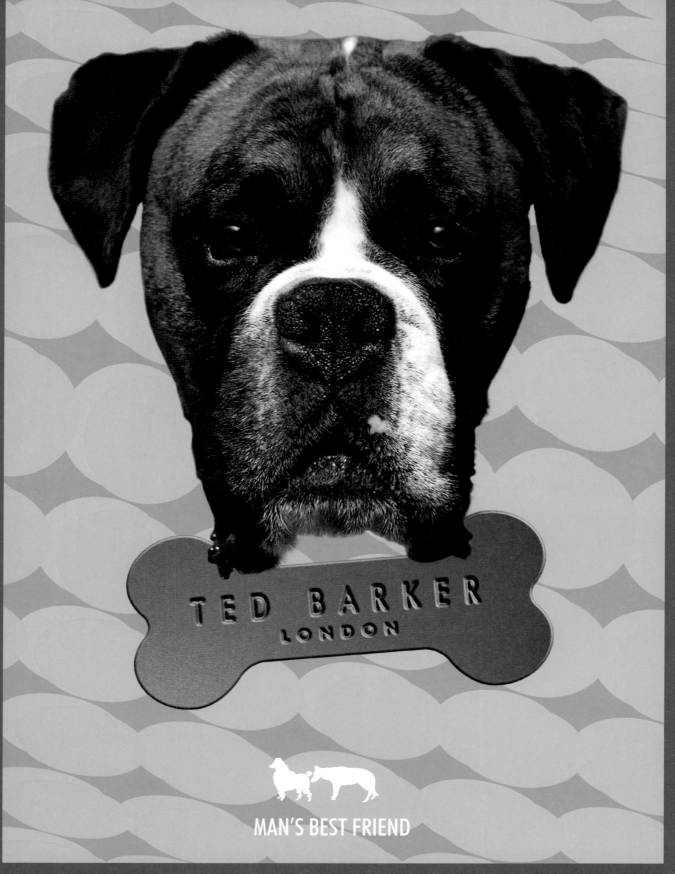

TIME: 12.43
DATE:1.10.95

I ♥ STYLOROUGE

#THEIR INNOVATION
SHINES...
IN AN ABILITY
TO TURN
#MUNDANE
EVERYDAY
IMAGES FROM...
THE HIGH STREET
INTO...
#IRONIC CULTURAL..
COMMENTS.- I.D.
£..

THANK YOU
PLEASE CALL AGAIN

THE BRILLIANT GREEN

BYE BYE
MR MUG

The Brilliant Green
Bye Bye Mr Mug
Single

OPPOSITE
Ted Baker
Instore Point of Sale

The aim of this point-of-sale
campaign was to draw more
attention to Ted Baker's growing
womenswear range, albeit in
typically obtuse fashion (and as usual
without showing the actual clothes).
Our observation that we
see certain breeds of dog as being
either 'boys' or 'girls' gave rise to
this poster series of canine portraits
(three 'boys', three 'girls').

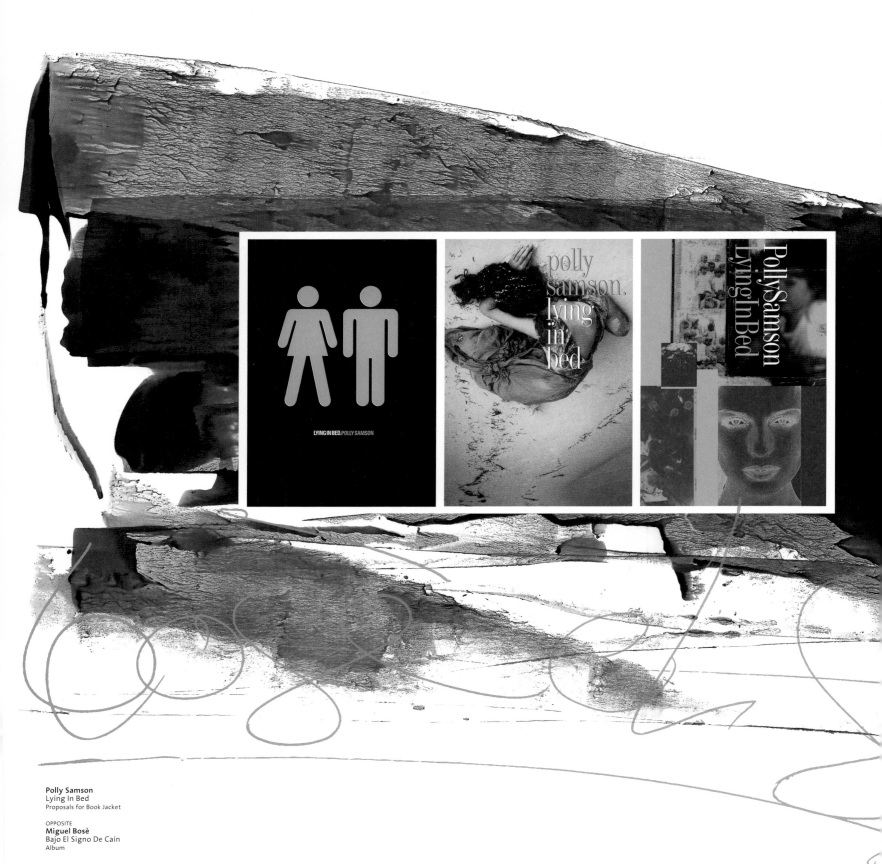

LYING IN BED. POLLY SAMSON

polly
samson,
lying
in
bed

PollySamson
LyingInBed

Polly Samson
Lying In Bed
Proposals for Book Jacket

OPPOSITE
Miguel Bosè
Bajo El Signo De Caín
Album

bajo el Signo de \ Caín...

bose

01. **11 to fly** {radio edit} 3.33 02. **11 to fly** {bel air rick mix} 7.55 03. **here's where the story ends** {canny remix} 6.11
tracks 01 & 02 written by l.edwards, d.stokes, w.page. produced by tin tin out. vocals by wendy page. guitar & keyboards by lindsay edwards. strings by the duke quartet. strings arranged by john metcalfe. percussion by preston hayman. bass by marcus cliffe. additional vocal arrangement by lawrence johnson. published by emi music, chrysalis music. choir provided by tuff sessions c/o lawrence johnson. remix on track 02 by dean thatcher & gary burns for shyone horse. ℗ 1999 virgin records ltd. track 03 written by wheeler, gavurin. remix & additional production by canny. mixed & produced by tin tin out. vocals by shelley nelson. published by warner chappell music ltd. mcps. ℗ 1998 virgin records ltd. design by stylorouge. photography by simon fowler. vcrd52. © 1999 virgin records ltd. this label copy information is the subject of copyright protection. all rights reserved. © 1999 virgin records ltd. printed in the e.u.

tintinout

The challenging nature of the music produced by highly respected keyboard player Moraz and percussionist Bruford suggested sparring as much as jamming – This aerial photograph sees the two musicians partaking in their first judo experience.

OPPOSITE
Tin Tin Out
Eleven To Fly
Single Poster

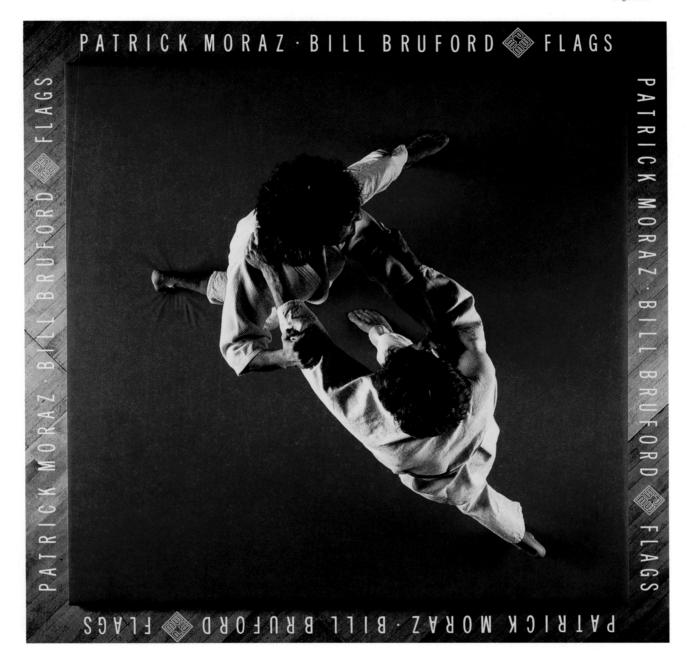

James
seven

Got to keep awake to what is happening
I can't see a thing through my ambition. I no
longer feel my God is watching over me.
Got to tell the world we've been dreaming.
This is not the end, a new beginning. I no
longer feel my God is watching over me.

GOLDCREST in association with THE NATIONAL FILM FINANCE CORPORATION presents

ANOTHER COUNTRY

15

With RUPERT EVERETT · Music by MICHAEL STOREY · Executive Producers ROBERT FOX JULIAN SEYMOUR
Screenplay by JULIAN MITCHELL Based on his original play · Produced by ALAN MARSHALL · Directed by MAREK KANIEVSKA

Convention outraged...
A class abandoned...
A country betrayed...

Another Country
Film poster

A re-creation of the dormitory set from the movie forms the appropriate background for this shot of leading man Rupert Everett.
The movie tells the story of one man's political and sexual subversion. The client's view: "It says it all – 'Fuck you, and fuck me' "

OPPOSITE
James
Seven
Album front and images from the inside packaging

This cover was inspired by the band's description of themselves – as a group of seven distinctly different personalities – and the pregnancy of one of the band member's partners. The imagery on the front and inner sleeve explores the themes of identity and personal development.

3586
TAPESTRY

Honeycrack
Sitting At Home
Single

OPPOSITE
Honeycrack
King Of Misery
Single

Go Away
Single

Prozaic
Album

Delicious.190

"Television is more interesting than people. If it were not we should have people standing in the corner of our rooms"

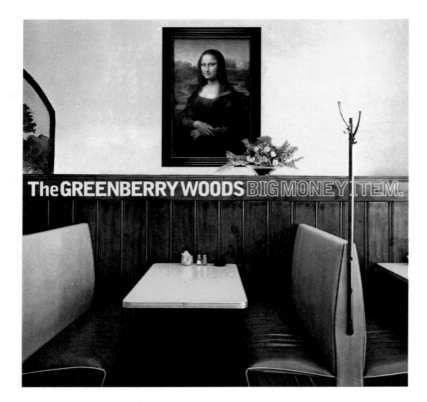

Greenberry Woods
Big Money Item
Album (front and inside images)

Greenberry Woods
Smash Up
Single

OPPOSITE
Catatonia
Mae Catatonia Yn
Dod O Gaerdyd
Page from Stylorouge
postcard book based on
design for Muller & Scully
single by Catatonia

mae
cananonia
yn
bod
o
caerdydd

From left to right:

Love And Money
Dogs In The Traffic
Album

The Darling Buds
Tiny Machine
Single

The Darling Buds
Bates
Proposal for Single

The Darling Buds
Crystal Clear
Single

Jocasta
Go
Single

Raw Stylus
Pushing Against The Flow
Single

RAWSTYLUS
PUSHING AGAINST THE FLOW

jocasta

the darling buds

WIRED 1234 WIRED RECORDINGS   RAW STYLUS PUSHING AGAINST THE FLOW

A Life Less Ordinary
Proposals for a series of
teaser posters as part of a
movie campaign

OPPOSITE
Geri Halliwell
Schizophonic
Album Packaging

GERI HALLIWELL SCHIZO-
PHONIC

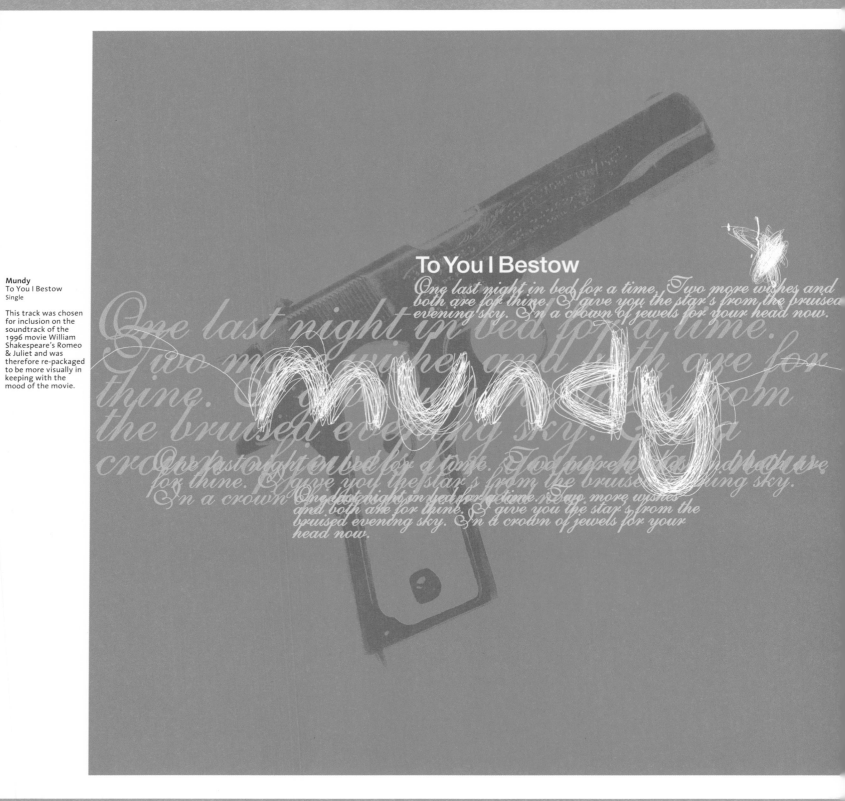

To You I Bestow

Mundy
To You I Bestow
Single

This track was chosen for inclusion on the soundtrack of the 1996 movie William Shakespeare's Romeo & Juliet and was therefore re-packaged to be more visually in keeping with the mood of the movie.

One last night in bed for a time. Two more wishes and both are for thine. I give you the star's from the bruised evening sky. In a crown of jewels for your head now.

One last night in bed for a time. Two more wishes and both are for thine. I give you the star's from the bruised evening sky. In a crown of jewels for your head now.

mundy

diesel park west

Diesel Park West
Shakespeare Alabama
Album

Both literary and
literal, two worlds
collide. Shakespeare
and the Mississippi
Delta are used to
illustrate the band's
Midlands roots and
their musical
influences in a 14
colour screenprint.
It proved easier to
buy a gecko than hire
one for the
photoshoot of the
finished print. He
remained the
photographer's pet
for four years.

Shakespeare
Alabama

State of **Flux**

by Rob O'Connor

Designers and teachers of design talk a lot about problem solving. I have no axe to grind over their use of the word solving, I do however have a small, er, problem with the word problem. Design is clearly a process that creates solutions, but to think of a problem as its source is an entirely negative concept to me. The biggest and most consistent cause of problems in my experience as a designer is humankind – people – people with opinions, with bosses, personal agendas, low aesthetic values, unsophisticated or just downright bad taste, obsessions with lowest-common-denominator marketing, lack of imagination, lack of self-confidence, little respect for the design profession, a low propensity for telling the truth, a lack of communication skills, no practical experience, no sense of bravery (or, god forbid, no sense of humour).

Don't get me wrong here, my soapbox is tucked well under the desk – this is not a tirade against the world at large. What breeds successful design is respect and patronage. Fortunately, we have had the opportunity to work for a handful of people who have shown us both. The best designer in the world will struggle working for an uncreative and uncooperative client. (Strangely enough, they do exist). What fires creative output is a stimulating relationship with the commissioner based on trust and a mutual respect. Much of our own work has come from one of the biggest risk businesses around – the music industry. It offers no guarantees of success, so risks have to be taken to convince an increasingly fickle market (and the rest of the industry) that any one particular musical artist has a truly unique talent, style, sound, attitude, whatever. The overriding tendency, though, is to play safe with the marketing approach – to make sure the artist or project is pigeonholed enough to not be misunderstood by the market and, as a consequence, passed over.

At the time of writing, the retail sector of the music industry is in a state of flux. For so many recent years major retail chains have held a whip hand high over the music business, forcing out the artists with something original to say; sending them underground, into the specialist shops, on to the Internet, on to the dole. There is just not enough room or profitability in stocking more than the most popular

Hipkiss
Raw Love
Image from single/album campaign

OPPOSITE
Stylorouge
Video stills
Images from promo videos, commercials and TV programmes for:
Ronny Jordan, Enya, Maxi Priest, Kula Shaker, Squeeze, Kirsty MacColl, Yu-ra, Vangelis, Show of Hands, Feeder, Your Generation, All About Eve, Crowded House, Simple Minds, Johnny Panic, NME Brats Awards.

music available, so the shops opt for selling more copies of less titles – the obvious chart big-hitters. As a consequence, the major record companies mould their roster of artists to suit this genre-based, copycat system. If they can't get their music played on mainstream radio (think of radio here as the other whip hand) then exposure in the shops is paramount, thereby convincing the record buying browser that if they like Sheryl Crow, Oasis or TLC then they'd like this, this or this ("go on, pick it up – it looks familiar to you, surely").

Marketing drives the visual media within the industry, with obvious reason, but when every so often a truly independent spirit enters the arena – a 4AD, a Stiff, a Mute, a Factor – the industry and the music-loving world at large applauds as well they might. The struggle to be truly creative – even in the area of design, is helped by the team ethic. The shared vision permeates these companies and reflects their less-compromised stand. All designers covet this shared-vision approach to creating an image. They don't really want to

spend valuable time and effort cajoling and coercing a stubborn mainstream marketeer into adopting a more original and adventurous design route when that time could be spent exploring those very same creative possibilities.

Designing 'record' sleeves is punctuated by little victories – smaller, more interesting type, pictures of the artist relegated to the inside of the package, a modicum of imagination behind the main image… is it so much to ask? After all, this is the career that used be known as 'commercial art', is it not?

The temptation is often for the designer to be bloody-minded, but common sense normally prevails. After all, if we are to do our job properly, we must accept that the careers of the music makers themselves rely on turning a profit from the sales of their music (and ours in turn from those very same sales).

The playing field has changed dramatically in music design). If anything, the goal posts have been pulled closer – the record

タイルの視覚化

companies' determination not to fail have given everyone less room to be creative – the future appears to be the wide open spaces of the Internet – multiple audio and video opportunities to cater for all tastes. From the designer's point of view, the record sleeve's evolution from a playground of visual fantasy to mini poster continues as the internet turns us all into film makers, publishers, multimedia artists. Our beloved record cover will fulfil its course and become merely the central brand image at the core of a multimedia marketing campaign. Real high street visibility for the pop music protagonists may soon rely solely on the PR machinery that puts pop star with film star in romantic tabloid front-page photo opportunities, and a handful of self-publicists may eclipse the multitude of other musical creatives even further into obscurity, but perhaps the Internet is the natural home for less fame-hungry music makers. There they can build their profile more on their own terms, however esoteric this may appear to be – they'll still be able to play their music live (won't they?).

Perhaps the industry has tried to make celebrities of ordinary Joes for too long – after all, musical genius shouldn't have to be accompanied by an overgrown ego, a beautiful face and a curvaceous body (was Mozart cute?). Imagery will always go hand in hand with sound – the pop video continues to thrive, the movie soundtrack is as potent a force as ever. The record sleeve as visual interpreter has passed its prime but it will continue to protect its increasingly less fragile contents all the while the market so dictates.

The visual potential for music continues to grow in much more liberating media – more movement, more interactivity, more stimulation.

The 1970s, Eighties and Nineties exposed the talents of Roger Dean, John Kosh, Hipgnosis, V23, M&Co, Assorted Images and others during music packaging's purple patch. None of them will be looking back at it through a rosy mist of nostalgia – the future is far too exciting.

Jimi Hendrix
The Ultimate Experience
Book Spreads

OPPOSITE
Spear Of Destiny
Was That You?
Poster for single

The Blue Nile
Saturday Night
Single

Pooka
Pooka
Album (back cover)

THE CREATURES · MISS THE GIRL

The Creatures
Miss The Girl
Single

The Creatures
Feast
Album

OPPOSITE

Hipkiss
Raw Love
Proposed image for single

Menswear
Being Brave
Single Poster

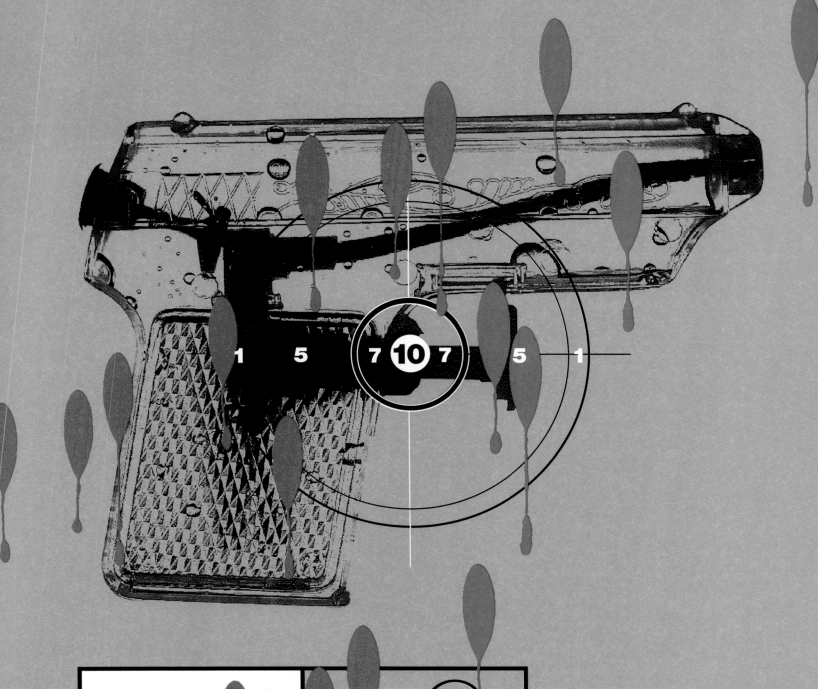

mens we@r

being brave the new single out march 4

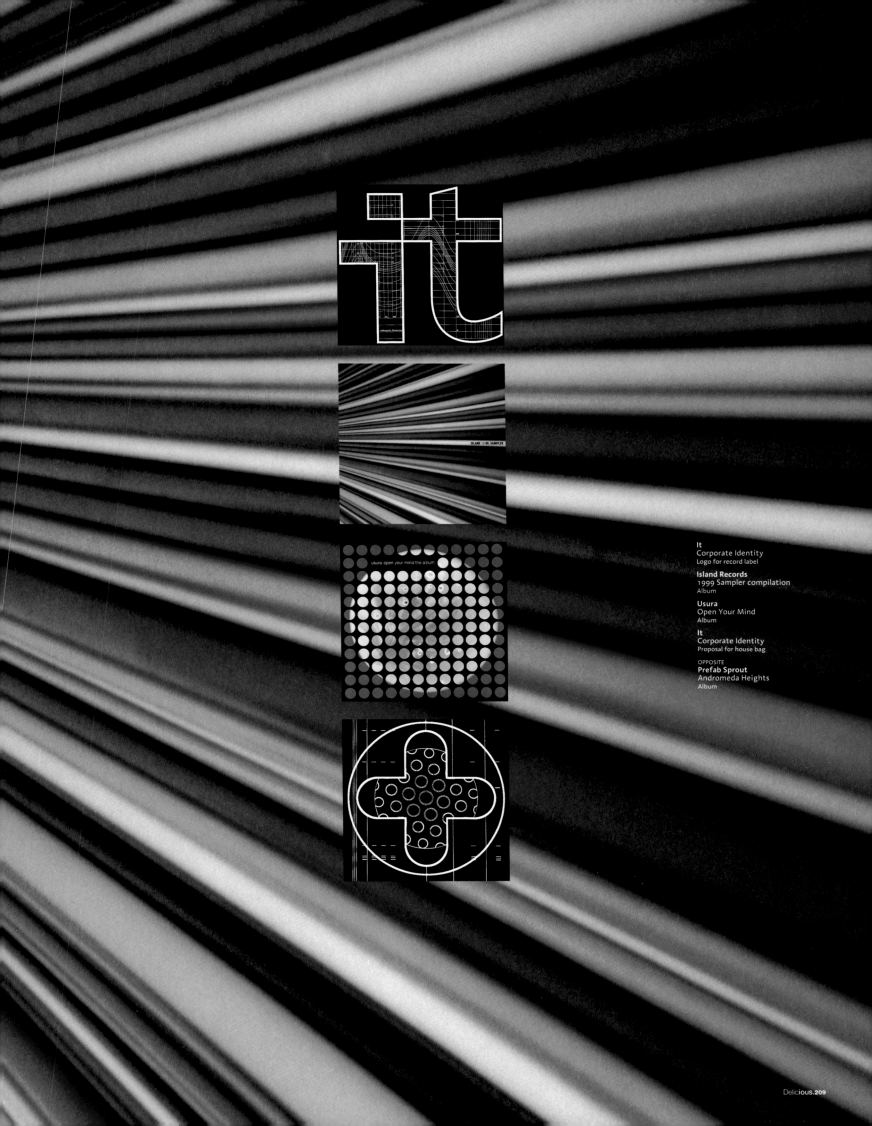

It
Corporate Identity
Logo for record label

Island Records
1999 Sampler compilation
Album

Usura
Open Your Mind
Album

It
Corporate Identity
Proposal for house bag

OPPOSITE
Prefab Sprout
Andromeda Heights
Album

OPPOSITE

Excellent Cadavers
Proposal for HBO film poster
The film was eventually
titled Falcone

Playlouder
Corporate identity for an
alternative music and lifestyle
website, background images
created for the look and feel of
the site, and an Invitation to the
launch party

OPPOSITE
Octopus
From A to B
Album packaging

The brief was to produce an album
cover that evoked the feeling of
an old-fashioned compendium of
games. The title, From A to B, was
adopted as a theme for a board
game involving a journey, where
the player confronts both
practical and emotional obstacles.
The fold out game takes about 4
minutes to play (the same length
of time it takes to hear the album)

Octopus
Saved
Illustrations for single packaging

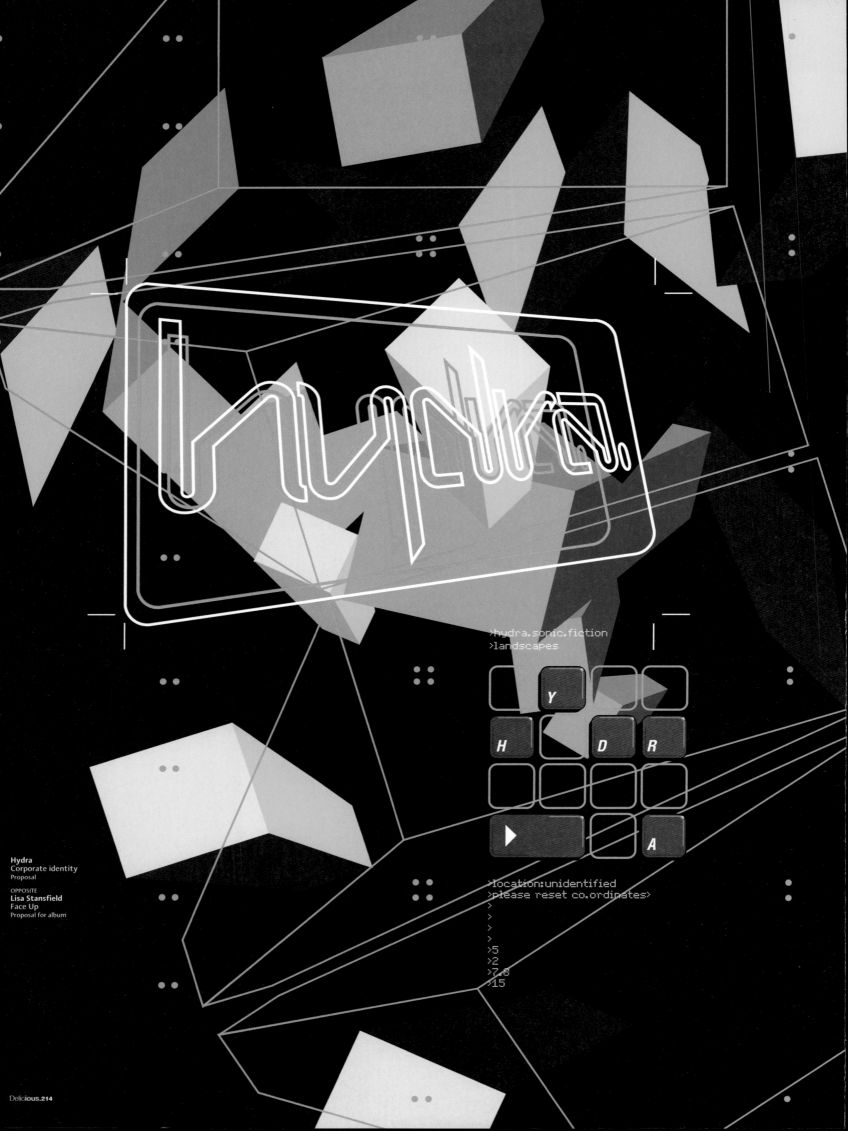

>hydra.sonic.fiction
>landscapes

Hydra
Corporate identity
Proposal

OPPOSITE
Lisa Stansfield
Face Up
Proposal for album

>location:unidentified
>please reset co.ordinates>
>
>
>
>5
>2
>7.8
>15

LISA STANSFIELD
face up

00 / 01

08 / 09

16 / 17

24 / 25

02 / 03

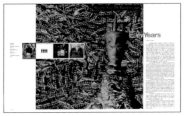

10 / 11

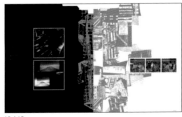

18 / 19

26 / 27

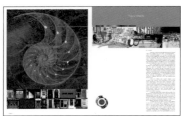

04 / 05

12 / 13

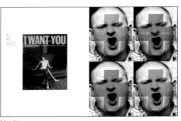

20 / 21

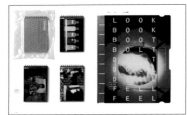

28 / 29

06 / 07

14 / 15

22 / 23

30 / 31

01
Illustration: Allan Stone

02 / 03
Ingredients
Editorial illustration: Sound On The Internet
Illustration: Robin Chenery
1998 MacUser

04 / 05
We Know Where You Live
Stylorouge Corporate ID
Photography: Lisa Sowray/Pictor International
Map: reproduced by permission of Geographer's
A-Z Map Co. Ltd. License no. B1060.
This product includes mapping data licensed from
Ordnance Survey ®.
© Crown Copyright 2001. License no. 100017302.

06 / 07
The Creatures Wild Things (EP)
Photography: Adrian Boot
1981 Polydor Records

08 / 09
Orange Juice Lean Period (single)
1984 Polydor Records

10 / 11
Siouxsie And The Banshees juju (album)
Photo-illustration: Thomi Wroblewski
1981 Polydor Records

Bob Marley Album box set
Photography: Adrian Boot /Chris Craske
1982 Island Records

Siouxsie And The Banshees Join Hands (album)
Photography: Adrian Boot
1979 Polydor Records

The Wanderers Only Lovers Left Alive (album)
Photography: Michael Beal
1981 Polydor Records

The Chords Maybe Tomorrow (single)
1980 Polydor Records

12 / 13
'Self portrait' of Rob O'Connor
Photography: Simon Fowler
1985

Killing Joke Revelations (album)
Photography: Trevor Rogers
1982 EG/Polydor Records

Killing Joke Love Like Blood (single)
Photography: Jeff Veitch
1985 EG/Polydor Records

Orange Juice Texas Fever (mini album)
Photography: Robert Sharp
1984 Polydor Records

The Stranglers European Female (single)
Photography: Jeff Veitch
1982 Epic Records

Iain Sutherland Mixed Emotions (album)
1983 Avatar Records

Sham 69 The First The Best And The Last (album)
Photography: Rob O'Connor
1980 Polydor Records

Killing Joke Ha (mini album)
1982 EG/Polydor Records

Wham! Bad Boys (single)
Photography: Chris Craymer
1983 Epic Records

14 / 15
Adam Ant Vive Le Rock (album)
Photography: Nick Knight
1985 CBS/Sony Records

Killing Joke Sanity (single)
Photography: Marion Schult/Cindy Palmano
1986 EG/Polydor Records

16 / 17
The Passions I'm In Love With A German Film Star (single)
Illustration: Rose Harrison
1981 Polydor Records

Siouxsie And The Banshees Spellbound (poster)
Illustration: Lars and Lois Hokansen
1980 Polydor Records

Siouxsie And The Banshees Israel (single)
Illustration: Chris Moore
1980 Polydor Records

Siouxsie And The Banshees Christine (single)
Photography: Paddy Eckersley
1980 Polydor Records

Shriekback Fish Below The Ice (single)
Photography: Nick Yates
1985 Arista Records

Music For Pleasure Light (single)
Photography: Rick Mann
1982 Polydor Records

Music For Pleasure Time (single)
1983 Polydor Records

Music For Pleasure Into The Rain (album)
1982 Polydor Records

18 / 19
Scott Walker Tilt (album)
Photography: David Scheinmann
1997 Polydor Records

Echo And The Bunnymen Rust (promo single)
Photography: Photonica
1999 London Records

Wildflowers The New York Jazz Loft Sessions
(compilation albums) Stock photography
1995 Douglas Records

20 / 21
Salad I Want You (poster)
Photography: Andy Earl
1996 Island/Universal Records

Soul II Soul Represent (poster for single)
Photography: Regan Cameron
1997 Island/Universal Records

22 / 23
Stylorouge Perestroika website pages
Background photography: Rob O'Connor
1996

Perestroika screensaver grabs
Photography: Robin Chenery, Rob O'Connor,
Gavin Evans, Julian Quayle
1996

24 / 25
Page 24
Photography: Lisa Sowray/Rob O'Connor
1998

Seven Stranger Than Fiction (poster for single)
Photography: Neil Kirk
1984 Polydor Records

26 /27
Nik Kershaw The Works (album)
Photography: Nic Georghiou
1989 MCA Records

Lili Marleen Soundtrack (album)
Illustration: Rose Harrison
1982 Metropolis/Island Records

Inge Van Hendrick Switch Me On (images for album)
Photography: Joseph Hunwick
2000 Recognition Records

28 / 29
Stylorouge Postcard book
Still-life photography: Nigel Schermuly
1999

Ted Baker Skinwear fragrance range packaging
Photography: Jason Tozer
1998

Beverley Knight CD packaging
Photography: Tim Bret-Day
1998 Parlophone

Fevertree Publicity material
Photography: Simon Fowler
1998

Stylorouge Look-Feel
Photography: Merton Gauster
1998

30 / 31
Baby Chaos Ignoramous (single)
3D render: Fletcher
1996 East West Records

The Passions Thirty Thousand Feet Over China
(images from album)
Photography: Jeff Veitch
1981 Polydor Records

32 / 33

40 / 41

48 / 49

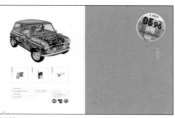
56 / 57

34 / 35

42 / 43

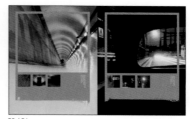
50 / 51

58 / 59

36 / 37

44 / 45

52 / 53

60 / 61

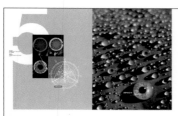
38 / 39

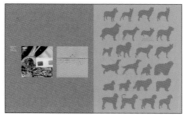
46 / 47

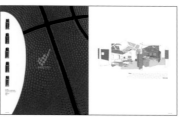
54 / 55

62 / 63

64 / 65

66 / 67

68 / 69

70 / 71

72 / 73

64 / 65
Longpigs Mobile Home (album)
Photography: Nels Israelson
1999 Mother/Polydor Records

Longpigs The Frank Sonata (single)
Photography: Nels Israelson
1999 Mother/Polydor Records

Longpigs Blue Skies (single)
Photography: Nels Israelson
Other photography: Sheridan Wall
1999 Mother/Polydor Records

66 / 67
Food Recordings The Food Christmas EP
1989 EMI/Food Records

James Wah Wah (proposal for album)
1993 Phonogram/Mercury Records

Prick Up Your Ears Video inlay (back & front)
Illustration: Mark Caylor
1987 Virgin Vision

68 / 69
Scarlet Chemistry
Photography: Zanna
1996 Warner Music

Jesus Jones Scratched
Photography: Rob O'Connor
1993 EMI/Food Records

Hipkiss Bluebird
Photography: Michele Turriani
1997 Sony Records (Germany)

Ashley Maher Pomegranate
Photography: Joseph Hunwick
1991 Virgin Records

Echobelly Everyone's Got One
Photography: Maria Mochnacz
1994 Rhythm King Records

The Jesus and Mary Chain Come On
Images taken from promo video directed by Sophie Muller
1994 Warner Music

Baby Chaos Hello
Photography: Matthew Donaldson
1994 East West Records

Headswim Despite Yourself (album)
Photography: Caroline Greyshock
1997 Epic Records

Mike Lindup Conversations With Silence (album)
Photography: Mike Lindup
2001 Mike Lindup

Dawn Of Electronica Compilation
Photography: Rob O'Connor
2000 Demon Records

Taeko Onuki Drawing (album)
Photography: Rob O'Connor
1991 Toshiba/EMI Records

70 / 71
Miki Imai Pride (album)
Photography: Sheila Rock
1997 For Life Records Inc.

Menswear We Love You (single)
Photography: Simon Fowler
1996 London/Laurel Records

72 /73
Mick Karn Bestial Cluster (album)
Photography: Kevin Westenberg
1993 CMP Records

74 / 75
Mugshots (left to right, top to bottom)

Squeeze A Round And A Bout, Photography: Various, 1990
Act of Faith One Vision, Photography: Simon Fowler/Charlie Waite, 1995
Killing Joke Night Time, Photography: Jeff Veitch, 1985
The Escape Club Wild Wild West, Photography: Nels Israelson, 1988
Paul Young Calling You, Photography: The Douglas Brothers, 1990
Robert Hart Angel, Photography: Simon Fowler, 1992
Shriekback Big Night Music, Photography: Peter Ashworth, 1985
Jason Donovan All Around The World, Photography: Peter Mac, 1993
Princess All For Love, Photography: Tim O'Sullivan, 1987
Johnny Hates Jazz Shattered Dreams, Photography: Simon Fowler, 1987
Julian Lennon Now You're In Heaven, Photography: Sheila Rock, 1989
A-ha Headlines And Deadlines, Photography: Just Loomis, 1991
All About Eve Touched By Jesus, Photography: Simon Fowler/ Derek Berwin, 1991
Horse Careful, Photography: Richard Haughton, 1990
Dannii Minogue Love And Kisses, Photography: Paul Cox, 1991
Nick Heyward A Hard Days Nick, Photography: Lawrence Watson, 1996
Dalbello Talk To Me, Photography: Richard Haughton, 1987
Orchestral Manoeuvres In The Dark The Best Of OMD, Photography: Andrew Catlin, 1988
Belinda Carlisle A Woman And A Man, Photography: Ellen Von Unwerth,1996
Kid Creole And The Coconuts Don't Take My Coconuts, Illustration: Rose Harrison, 1982
Jepp Seven:Eleven, Photography: Gry Garness, 1999
The Pretenders Last Of The Independents, Photography: Simon Fowler, 1994
Orange Juice The Orange Juice, Photography: Alan Horne, 1984
The Mike Flowers Pops A Groovy Place, Photography: Antony Mark Briggs, 1996
Taeko Onuki Shooting Star In The Blue Sky, Photography: Simon Fowler, 1993
Clive Griffin Step By Step, Photography: John Stoddart, 1989
Judy Cheeks No Outsiders, Photography: Paul Cox, 1988
Sarah Brightman Fly, Photography: Simon Fowler, 1995
Mansun Negative, Photography: Pennie Smith, 1998
Tolu Divine, Photography: David Scheinmann, 1993
Squeeze Trust Me To Open My Mouth, Photography: Simon Fowler, 1987
The Darling Buds Sure Thing, Photography: Simon Fowler, 1992
Gregory Isaacs Cool Down The Pace, Photography: Jonnie Black, Illustration: Rose Harrison, 1982
James Laid, Photography: Kevin Westenberg, 1993
Del Amitri Be My Downfall, Photography: Kevin Westenberg, 1992
Raw Stylus Pushing Against The Flow, Photography: Phil Knott, 1995
Simple Minds Love Song/Alive And Kicking, Photography: Simon Fowler, 1992
Maxi Priest Close To You, Photography: Simon Fowler, 1990
Nik Kershaw One Step Ahead, Photography: Nic Georghiou, 1988
Skin Games The Bloodrush, Photography: Simon Fowler, 1989
Ronny Jordan Under Your Spell, Photography: Simon Fowler, 1993
Bliss I Hear You Call, Photography: The Douglas Brothers, 1989
Chris De Burgh This Silent World, Photography: c/o A & M, 1994
Howard Jones Two Souls, Photography: David Scheinmann, 1992
Sandy Denny Who Knows Where The Time Goes?, Photography: David Bailey, 1985
Richard Traviss Preacher, Photography: Julian Barton, 1994
Errol Brown Personal Touch, Photography: Sheila Rock, 1987
BeeGees Paying The Price Of Love, Photography: Andy Earl, 1993
Joan Armatrading Free, Photography: Richard Haughton, 1990
Skin Games Your Luck's Changed, Photography: Simon Fowler, 1989
Horse The Same Sky, Photography: Andy Catlin, 1990
Carmel Live In Paris, Photography: Alex Madjitey, 1997
Mundy Pardon Me, Photography: Adrian Green, 1997
Taeko Onuki Raindance (visual), Photography: Simon Fowler, 1993
Heaven West Eleven Album visual, Photography: Chris & Moggy, 1994
Simple Minds Real Life, Photography: Simon Fowler, 1991
Heather Small Proud, Photography: Nick Haddow, 2000
Placido Domingo From My Latin Soul, Photography: Simon Fowler, 1997
Chris Duffy All the Time In The World, Photography: Paul Cox, 1992
Eighth Wonder I'm Not Scared, Photography: Eamon J. McCabe, 1988
King Bitter Sweet, Photography: Simon Fowler, 1985
Mike Scott Building The City Of Light, Photography: Jill Furmanovsky, 1995
Ronny Jordan Come With Me, Photography: Simon Fowler, 1994
Blondie Atomic (The Best Of), Photography: Chrysalis Records, 1999
Go West Indian Summer, Photography: Nels Israelson, 1992
Diesel Park West Boy On Top Of The News, Photography: John Stoddart, 1991
Raw Stylus Believe In Me, Photography: Phil Knott, 1996
Ronny Jordan The Quiet Revolution, Photography: Simon Fowler, 1993
Dalbello Tango, Photography: Richard Haughton, 1987
Alabina Salam, Photography: Jay Alansky, 1999
Maxi Priest Crazy Love, Photography: Tansy Spinks, 1986
Mansun Being A Girl, Illustration: Pete Nevin, 1998
Lena Fiagbe Gotta Get It Right, Photography: Stephanie Rushton, 1993
Paul Young Oh Girl, Photography: The Douglas Brothers, 1991
Miki Imai Pride, Photography: Sheila Rock, 1997
Marvin Gaye The Very Best Of, Photography: c/o Motown, 1994
Voice Of The Beehive Perfect Place, Photography: Simon Fowler, 1991
Alison Moyet That Ole Devil Called Love, Photography: Simon Fowler, 1985
Merran See You Later, Photography: Sheila Rock, 1985
Steve Earle Johnny Come Lately, Photography: Pete Anderson, 1988
Ashley Maher Pomegranate, Photography: Joseph Hunwick, 1991
Orange Juice In A Nutshell, Illustration: Ian Wright, 1985
Ronny If You Want Me To Stay, Photography: Phil Jude, 1981
George Michael Father Figure, Photography: Brian Aris, 1987
Heaven West Eleven River Runs Dry, Photography: c/o Sony, 1994
Echo And The Bunnymen What Are You Going To Do With Your Life? Photography: Andrew Douglas, 1999
Maxi Priest Fe Real, Photography: Joseph Hunwick, 1992
Chris Sutton Chris Sutton, Photography: Simon Fowler, 1986
Echo And The Bunnymen Rust, Photography: Andrew Douglas, 1999
Julian Lennon You're The One, Photography: Sheila Rock, 1989
Sarah Brightman Dive, Photography: Simon Fowler, 1993
James Reyne Album, Photography: Richard Haughton, 1987
The Police Greatest Hits, Photography: Duane Michals, 1992
Howard New Straight To You, Photography: Andy Earl, 1997
Killing Joke Adorations, Photography: Cindy Palmano, 1986
Meatloaf Blind Before I Stop, Photography: Simon Fowler/ Trevor Rogers, 1986
Maxi Priest Some Guys Have All The Luck, Photography: Peter Ashworth, 1987
Tina Turner Two People, Photography: Paul Cox, 1986
Juice Can We Get Personal?, Photography: Simon Fowler, 1999
Dusty Springfield A Very Fine Love, Illustration: John Geary, 1995
Craig David Fill Me In, Photography: Mamad Mossedegh, 2000
Bob Marley And The Wailers Natural Mystic, Photography: Adrian Boot, 1985
Shed Seven A Maximum High, Photography: George Logan, 1996
Briana Corrigan Fool, Photography: Valerie Phillips, 1996
Saeko Suzuki Studio Romantic, Photography: Simon Fowler, 1987
David Cassidy The Last Kiss, Photography: Leon Lecash, 1985
All About Eve The Dreamer, Photography: Simon Fowler, 1991
Robert Fripp Network, Photography: Debbie Feingold, 1985
Level 42 A Physical Presence, Photography: Simon Fowler, 1985
Salvation Sunday Cold Grey Eyes, Photography: Simon Fowler, 1986
Beverley Knight Sista Sista, Photography: Sheila Rock, 1999
Jimi Hendrix Blues, Photography: Stock, 1994
Heaven West Eleven She's In Love, Photography: Eddie Monsoon, 1994
Cliff Richard Stronger, Photography: Trevor Rogers/Pirate Models, 1989
Alison Moyet Invisible, Photography: Simon Fowler, 1984
Voice Of The Beehive Honey Lingers, Photography: Pete Mountain, 1991
Del Amitri Waking Hours, Photography: Simon Fowler, 1990
Spear Of Destiny Strangers In Our Town, Illustration: Chris Welch, 1987
Salad Yeah,Yeah, Photography: Simon Fowler, 1997
Wild Weekend Who's Afraid Of The Big Bad Love?, Photography: Video stills by Chris Craske, 1990
Simple Minds Hypnotised, Photography: David Scheinmann, 1995
Donny Osmond Donny Osmond, Photography: Dean Freeman, 1988
Jason Donovan All Around The World, Photography: Peter Mac, 1993
Howard Jones Life In One Day, Photography: Panni Charrington/Simon Fowler, 1985
Stephen Gately New Beginning/Bright Eyes, Photography: Tim Bret-Day, 2000
Jean Louis Murat Le Manteau De Pluie, Photography: David Scheinmann, 1991
Shriekback Go Bang!, Photography: Simon Fowler, 1988
David Torn Tripping Over God, Photography: Rob O'Connor, 1995
Louise Goffin This Is The Place, Photography: Sheila Rock, 1988
Sandie Shaw Hello Angel, Photography: Peter Ashworth, 1988
Helen Hoffner Wild About Nothing, Photography: David Scheinmann, 1992
Joe Jackson Jumpin' Jive Live, Photography: Alexander W. Thomas 1998
Adam Ant Vive Le Rock, Photography: Mark Lebon, 1985
Taeko Onuki Drawing, Photography: Simon Fowler, 1991
The Sisters Of Mercy More, Photography: Marcus Tomlinson, 1990
Basia Time And Tide, Photography: Paul Cox, 1987
Sandie Shaw Are You Ready To Be Heartbroken?, Photography: Tansy Spinks, 1986
Bob Marley Iron, Lion, Zion, Photography: Adrian Boot, 1992
Belinda Carlisle Always Breaking My Heart, Photography: Lorenzo Agius, 1996
Maxi Priest Intentions, Photography: Tansy Spinks, 1986
The Chords So Far Away, Photography: Gered Mankowitz, 1980
Diesel Park West Like Princes Do, Photography: John Stoddart, 1989
Dum Dums You Do Something To Me, Photography: Martin Gardner, 2000
Voice Of The Beehive Monsters And Angels, Photography: Kevin Westenberg, 1991
Ruth Joy Pride And Joy, Photography: Eddie Monsoon, 1991
The Ramones I Wanna Be Sedated, Illustration: Paul Cemmick, 1980
Life's Addiction I Do Believe, Photo-illustration: Andy Huckle from portraits by Life's Addiction, 1997
Paul Young Tomb Of Memories, Photography: Simon Fowler, 1985
John Butler The Loyal Serpent, Photography: Stuart Weston, 1997
Ole Edvard Antonsen Read My Lips, Photography: Simon Fowler, 1998
Eighth Wonder Cross My Heart, Photography: Eamon J. McCabe, 1988
Mike Scott Bring 'Em All In, Photography: Stefano Giovannini, 1995
John Cale Music For A New Society, Photography: Bets Johnson, 1982
LA Mix We Shouldn't Hold Hands In The Dark, Photography: Simon Fowler, 1991
Del Amitri Change Everything, Photography: Kevin Westenberg, 1992
Tina Turner Break Every Rule, Photography: Herb Ritts, 1986
Johnny Hates Jazz Shattered Dreams, Photography: Simon Fowler, 1987
Simple Minds Stand By Love, Photography: Claude Gassian, 1991
Junior Tucker Love Is The Strongest Emotion, Photography: Russell Young, 1990
Jon Astley The Compleat Angler, Photography: Sheila Rock, 1988
Ashley Maher Hi, Photography: Victoria Pearson Cameron, 1990
Tom Waits In The Neighborhood, Photography: Lynn Goldsmith, 1983
Cast All Change, Photography: Norman Watson, 1995
So Are You Sure, Photography: Paul Cox, 1988
Headswim Despite Yourself, Photography: Chris Floyd, 1998
Hothouse Flowers Give It Up, Photography: Pete Mountain, 1990
Spear of Destiny Outland, Illustration: Chris Welch, 1987
Maxi Priest One More Chance, Photography: David Scheinmann, 1993
Simple Minds Real Life, Photography: Simon Fowler, 1991
Voice Of The Beehive Scary Kisses, Photography: Joseph Hunwick, 1995
Meat Loaf Blind Before I Stop, Photography: Simon Fowler, 1986
Kiss Like This Faith In You, Photography: Simon Fowler, 1990
Love And Money My Love Lives In A Dead House Photography: Gavin Evans, 1991
Helen Hoffner Summer Of Love, Photography: David Scheinmann, 1992
Act of Faith Lost On A Breeze, Photography: Simon Fowler/ Charlie Waite, 1995
Maxi Priest Groovin' In The Midnight, Photography: Joseph Hunwick, 1992
Luke Goss And The Band Of Thieves Give Me One More Chance Photography: Simon Fowler, 1993
Zucchero Diamante, Photography: Terry O'Neill, 1990
Terence Trent D'Arby If You Let Me Stay, Photography: Sony Music, 1987
Sarah Brightman Captain Nemo, Photography: Simon Fowler, 1993
Buddy Curtess And The Grasshoppers Bridge Over Troubled Water Photography: Mike Prior, 1987
Cast Finetime, Photography: Lawrence Watson, 1995
Betsy Cook Love Is The Groove, Photography: Kate Garner, 1991
Enya A Day Without Rain, Photography: Sheila Rock, 2000
The Cure Bloodflowers, Photography: Robert Smith, 2000
Bliss How Does It Feel The Morning After?, Photography: The Douglas Brothers, 1989

76 / 77

84 / 85

92 / 93

100 / 101

78 / 79

86 / 87

94 / 95

102 / 103

80 / 81

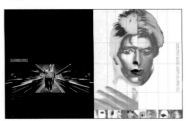

88 / 89

96 / 97

104 / 105

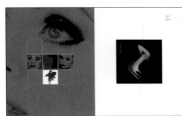

82 / 83

90 / 91

98 / 99

106 / 107

76 / 77
George Michael Faith (album)
Photography: Russell Young
1987 Epic Records

Geri Halliwell Look At Me (poster campaign)
Photography: Dean Freeman
1999 EMI/Chrysalis Records

78/ 79
Adam Ant Apollo 9 (poster)
Photography: Mark Lebon
1984 CBS/Sony Records

Blur Leisure (album)
Photography: Hulton Picture Co.
1991EMI/Food Records

Picnic At The Whitehouse Success (single)
Photography: Cindy Palmano/Trevor Rogers
1987 Portrait/CBS Records

80 / 81
Lena Fiagbe Visions (image from album packaging)
Photography: Marcus Tomlinson
1994 Mother Records

Angel Pie She/Tinfoil Valley (single images)
Photography: Simon Fowler
1994 Oxygen Records

82 / 83
Sarah Brightman Surrender (album images)
Photography: Simon Fowler
1992 Polydor Records

Landmark Album box set
1999 London Records

84
Paradise Lost Host (album images)
Photography: Paul Postle
1999 EMI Records Germany

85
Paradise Lost Icon (album images)
Photography: Matt Anker
1993 Music For Nations

Paradise Lost Seals The Sense (single images)
Photography: Matt Anker/Rob O'Connor
1994 Music For Nations

86 / 87
Visuals
Including photography by: Trevor Rogers, Rob O'Connor,
Rob Chenery and illustration by Jamie Hewlett

88 /89
Dum Dums I Can't Get You Out Of My Thoughts (single)
Photography: Andy Earl (background: Martin Gardner)
2000 Wildstar Records

David Bowie The Best Of (albums)
Photography left: Mick Rock right: Steve Schapiro
1998 EMI Records

90 / 91
Shot Through The Heart Proposal for film poster
Photography from production stills supplied by distributor
1987 Palace Pictures

Thelonious Monk – Straight No Chaser
Proposal for film poster
Photography: shot from video by Chris Craske
1989 Warner Pictures

Edward II Proposal for film poster
Photography from production stills supplied by distributor
1991 Palace Pictures

Parker Film poster
Photography from production stills supplied by distributor
1980 Virgin Vision

Kula Shaker K (album)
Illustration: Dave Gibbons
1996 Columbia Records

92 / 93
Superphenix (album)
Photography: Simon Fowler
1998 TriStar/Sony France

94 / 95
The Poets Welcome To The Heathen Reserve (album)
Photography: David Scheinmann
Illustration: Mark Caylor
1993 EMI/Medley Records

Albert Camus The Outsider (book jacket proposal)
Photography: Tony Hung
Still-life photography: Nigel Schermuly
1998 Penguin Books

96 / 97
FFF Blast Culture (album)
Photography: Stephane Sedanoui
Screenprint: Chris Thomson/Karl Scholes
1991 Sony Records France

Pictor Photographic library advertising
Photography: Pictor
1997-98 Pictor

98 / 99
Simple Minds Good News From The Next World (album images)
Photography: David Scheinmann/Rob O'Connor/Stuart Mackenzie
1995 Virgin Records

100 / 101
Raw Sex, Pure Energy Stop The War (single)
Image: Stock
1982 Island/Universal Records

Twin Town Film poster
Photography: Lorenzo Agius
1997 PolyGram Records

Shed Seven Going For Gold (single)
Photography: Simon Fowler
1996 Polydor Records

Strangelove Hysteria Unknown (single)
Video stills by Julian Poole
1992 EMI/Food Records

Octopus Your Smile (single)
Photography: Simon Fowler
1996 EMI/Food Records

UB40 Kingston Town (single)
Painting: Barry Kamen
1990 Virgin/DEP Records

Life's Addiction Jesus Coming In For The Kill (single)
Illustration: Andy Huckle
1997 London Records

The Wall Dirges And Anthems (album)
Photography: Paddy Eckersley
1981 Polydor Records

102 / 103
Blur Starshaped (image for video packaging)
Photography: Trevor Rogers
1995 PMI/Food Records

104 / 105
Blur Popscene (single)
Photography: David Grewcock
1992 EMI/Food Records

Blur Leisure (album)
Photography: Hulton Picture Co.
1991 EMI/Food Records

Blur Girls And Boys (single)
Photography: Barnaby's
1994 EMI/Food Records

Blur Bang (single)
Photography: Quantity
1991 EMI/Food Records

Blur For Tomorrow (single)
Illustration: Paul Stephens
1993 EMI/Food Records

Blur There's No Other Way (single)
Photography: Hulton Picture Co.
1991 EMI/Food Records

Blur Sunday Sunday (single)
Illustration: Scott Wilson
1993 EMI/Food Records

Blur Parklife (album)
Brunskill/Bob Thomas
1994 EMI/Food Records

106 / 107
Blur Parklife (visual)
Photography: Barnaby's
1994 EMI/Food Records

Blur End Of A Century (single)
Photography: Trevor Webb, John Mac (logo type)
1994 EMI/Food Records

Blur She's So High/I Know (single)
Painting: Mel Ramos
1990 EMI/Food Records

Blur Stereotypes (single)
Photography: Tony Stone
1996 EMI/Food Records

Blur Image for Collectors' Edition album (Japan)
Illustration: John Geary
EMI/Food

Blur Parklife (single)
Photography: Barnaby's
1996 EMI/Food Records

Blur The Universal (single)
Photography: The Telegraph Picture Library
1995 EMI/Food

Blur Country House (single)
Photography: The Telegraph Picture Library
1995 EMI/Food Records

Blur Blurbook (book cover)
Photography: Paul Postle
1995 Harper Collins

108 / 109

116 / 117

124 / 125

132 / 133

110 / 111

118 / 119

126 / 127

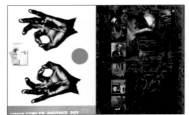

134 / 135

112 / 113

120 / 121

128 / 129

136 / 137

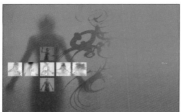

114 / 115

122 / 123

130 / 131

138 / 139

108 / 109
Blur She's So High/I Know (poster for single)
Painting: Mel Ramos
Photograph: Chris Craske
1990 EMI/Food Records

Blur The Great Escape (packaging)
Photography: Pictor (left), Nels Israelson (right)
1995 EMI/Food

110 / 111
Blur Miscellaneous
Various (with thanks to Barnaby's and
Michael Woodward Licencing)

Blur The Great Escape (album)
Photography: Tom King/The Image Bank
1995 EMI/Food Records

112 / 113
Blur Girls And Boys (single visual)
Photography: Barnaby's
1994 EMI/Food

Dr John Anutha Zone (album)
Photography: Andy Earl
1998 Parlophone Records

114 / 115
Yura Beyond The Pale (album images)
Photography: Glen Erler
1998 Ki/oon Sony Records Japan

116 / 117
Headswim images for Tourniqué (single) & Despite Yourself
(album), Photography: Caroline Greyshock/Julian Quayle
1997 Epic Records

118 / 119
Joan Armatrading Hearts And Flowers (album cover)
Photography: Richard Haughton
1990 A&M/Universal Records

Paddy Casey Amen (So Be It) (album visual)
Photography: Katerina Jebb
1999 Sony Records

Richard Thompson Mock Tudor (album)
Illustration: Paul Slater
1999 Capitol Records (USA)

Kula Shaker Tattva (single)
1996 Columbia Records

Shack HMS Fable (album)
Screenprint: Andy Huckle
1999 London Records

120 / 121
Fashion Forums Poster Image
Photography: Marcus Wilson-Smith
1985 Banks Sadler

Redtape Music From The Third Floor (CBS promotional album)
Illustration: Mark Caylor

122 / 123
Stylorouge T-shirt designs

124 / 125
Danielle Dax Blast The Human Flower (album back)
Photography: Simon Fowler
1990 Sire/WEA Records (USA)

Danielle Dax Blast The Human Flower (album front)
Photography: Simon Fowler, bullets by Trevor Rogers
1990 Sire/WEA Records (USA)

126 / 127
Photography: Nigel Schermuly
2001

Elvis Presley Proposal for exhibition poster
Copyright of Elvis Presley Enterprises Inc.
1993 Exhibit A/Elvis Presley Enterprises Inc.

128 / 129
Kinky Machine Kinky Machine (album)
Photography: Jack Daniels
1993 Oxygen Records

Kinky Machine Going Out With God (single)
Photography: Jack Daniels
1993 Oxygen Records

Kinky Machine Shockaholic (single)
Photography: Jack Daniels
1993 Oxygen Records

Jesus Jones Already (album)
Illustration: Blaise Thompson
1997 EMI/Food Records

130 / 131
logos

Siouxsie and the Banshees Once Upon A Time
(poster/album)
Video stills by Rick Mann
1981 Polydor Records

132 / 133
Celebration (page from Stylorouge promotional book)
featuring Liquidizer (album)
Photography: Trevor Rogers
1989 EMI/Food Records

Jesus Jones Info Psycho (single)
Photography: Simon Fowler, 1989 EMI/Food Records
Doubt (album)
Illustration: David Calderley, 1991 EMI/Food Records
Proposal for special packaging, 1991 EMI/Food Records
Info Freako (single)
Photography: Simon Fowler, 1989 EMI/Food Records

Mike Edwards (of Jesus Jones)
Photography: Simon Fowler, 1991

134 / 135
Simon Fowler Photography Corporate ID
Photography: Simon Fowler
1995 Simon Fowler

Prima Diva Compilation album
Photography: Sheila Rock
1994 EMI Classics

Beethoven Symphonien 56 (album proposal)
1995 EMI Classics

Tchaikovsky Passion (album proposal)
EMI archive
1993 EMI Classics

Tchaikovsky The Dance Album
Photography: Sheila Rock
1993 EMI Classics

Emmanuel Pahud Flute Concertos
Photography: Simon Fowler
1999 EMI Classics

Roger Norrington Mozart Requiem
Photography: David Scheinmann
1992 EMI Classics

Cyrano Poster
Photography: Karl Grant
1991 Royal Opera House

Schumann/Schnittke Cello Concertos
Photography: Geoff Brightling
1992 EMI Classics

136 / 137
Kula Shaker Peasants, Pigs And Astronauts
(images from album)
Photography: Jeff Cottenden
1999 Columbia Records

138 / 139
Strangelove Visionary (EP)
Photography: Julian Poole
1992 EMI Food Records

Echo And The Bunnymen Rust (single)
Photography: Andrew Douglas
1999 London

Propellerheads/David Arnold/Shirley Bassey
On Her Majesty's Secret Service (single)
Photography: Robin Chenery
1997 East West Records

Momo Arabesque (album)
Photography: Mark Luscombe-Whyte
1999 Gut Records

Pink Floyd Dark Side Of The Moon 20th Anniversary Edition
(elements from album) with Storm Thorgesen, Background:
Hipgnosis, Photography: Chris Craske, 1993 EMI Records

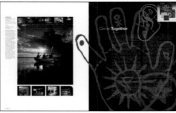

140 / 141

148 / 149

156 / 157

164 / 165

142 / 143

150 / 151

158 / 159

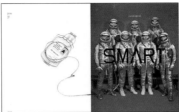

166 / 167

144 / 145

152 / 153

160 / 161

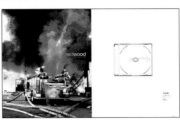

168 / 169

146 / 147

154 / 155

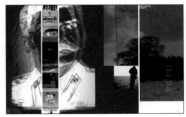

162 / 163

170 / 171

---

140 / 141
Crowded House Promotional shot from photo shoot
& images from Best Of campaign
Photography: Andy Earl
1996 Capitol/EMI Records

Crowded House Elements for Instinct (single) packaging
Illustration: Fred Vanhorenbeke
1996 Capitol/EMI Records

142 / 143
Straw Sailing Off The Edge Of The World (single proposal)
2000 Columbia Records

Blur Modern Life Is Rubbish (album)
Illustration (front): Michael Woodward Licencing
Illustration (back): Paul Stephens
1993 EMI/Food Records

144 / 145
The Blue Ox Babes Apples And Oranges (single)
Illustration: Mark Caylor
1998 Go! Discs

Helicopter Girl 345 Wonderful (single proposal)
Background Photograph: Photonica
2000 Instant Karma Records

146 / 147
Subcircus Images for Sixty Second Love Affair (single)
Photography: Michele Turriani
1999 Echo Records

A Moment On The Praha Metro
Photography: Robin Chenery
August 2000

148 / 149
Dave Stewart And Barbara Gaskin The Big Idea (album)
Photography: Geoff Brightling
1987 Broken Records

All About Eve What Kind Of Fool (single poster)
Photography: David Scheinmann
1988 Phonogram/Mercury Records

150 / 151
All About Eve Images from Strange Way (single)
Photography: Karl Grant / Simon Fowler
1991 Phonogram/Mercury Records

All About Eve The Dreamer (single proposal)
Still-life Photography: Karl Grant
1991 Phonogram/Mercury

All About Eve Images from Farewell Mr Sorrow (single)
Photography: Rob O'Connor
1991 Phonogram/Mercury Records

All About Eve Images from What Kind Of Fool
Photography: David Scheinmann
1988 Phonogram/Mercury Records

All About Eve Images from Scarlet And Other Stories
Photography: Holly Warburton
1991 Phonogram/Mercury Records

152 / 153
Rolling Stones No Security (press ad and album)
Photography: Zed Nelson, Snaps: Rob O'Connor
1998 Rolling Stones/Virgin Records

154 / 155
King Crimson Heartbeat (single)
1982 EG/Polydor Records

Lou Reed Retro (album)
Photography: RCA Archive
1989 BMG Records

Malcolm Mclaren Duck Rock Cheer
Photography: Trevor Rogers
1984 Virgin

Drizabone Conspiracy (album proposal)
Photography: Richard Croft
1995 Island/Universal Records

Latin Quarter Mick And Caroline (album)
Cover concept/photography: James Swinson, Additional
photography: courtesy of Colorific!, Barnaby's Picture Library,
Susan Meiselas, Magnum, S & G Press Agency Ltd.,
Syndication International
1987 Arista Records

Menswear Sleeping In (single ad)
Photography: London Records
1995 London/Laurel Records

Kula Shaker Hey Dude (single)
Photography: David Scheinmann
1996 Columbia Records

156 / 157
Pooka City Sick EP
Illustration: John Paul Early
1993 WEA Records

Baby Chaos Hello Victim (single)
Photography: Paul Rider
1994 East West Records

Alexei Sayle Albania! Albania!
The Albanian World Cup Squad (single)
Illustration: Graham Humphreys
1982 Island Records

Straw Keepsakes (album proposal)
2000 Columbia

Blancmange I Can See It (single)
Illustration: Mick Brownfield
1986 London Records

Echobelly On (album innersleeve imagery)
Including photos by Maria Mochnacz and Ray Burmiston
1995 Rhythm King Records

158 / 159
Squeeze Babylon And On (album poster)
Photography: Rex Features
1987 A&M/Universal Records

Squeeze Hourglass (single)
Illustration: David Calderley
1987 A&M/Universal Records

Squeeze 853 5937 (single)
Illustration: David Calderley
1987 A&M/Universal Records

Squeeze The Waiting Game (single)
Illustration: Chris Welch
1987 A&M/Universal Records

Squeeze Footprints (single)
Illustration: David Calderley
1987 A&M/Universal Records

Squeeze Some Fantastic Place (single image)
Photography: Jill Furmanovsky
1993 A&M/Universal Records

160 / 161
Ted Baker World Leaders (in-store poster campaign)
Illustration: Rob Hefferin
1997 Ted Baker

Ted Baker Condom packet (point-of-sale)
Illustration: Rob Hefferin
Photographed by Nigel Schermuly
1998 Ted Baker

162 / 163
Buddy Curtess And The Grasshoppers Poster image
Photography: Mike Prior
Phonogram Records

Shack Comedy (single)
1999 London Records

People Get Ready Be My Friend (single)
Photography: Peter Calvin
1991 Produce Records

Lick My Summer 31 (single)
1996 Warner

Desert Eagle Discs The Eagle Has Landed (album)
Photography: Peter Anderson
1998 BMG

Van Morrison Best Of Volume 2 (album)
Photography: Simon Fowler
1993 Polydor Records

Squeeze Unplugged (cover of tour brochure)
Illustration: Craig Hopson
1998 Chiharu Tsukada

Prefab Sprout Andromeda Heights (album)
Illustration: Anne Magill
1997 Columbia Records

Chris Sheehan Out Of The Woods (album)
Photography: Kin Ho
1995 East West

164 / 165
The Balanescu Quartet Possessed (album)
Photography: Tim Simmons
1992 Mute Records

Cud Once Again (single)
Photography: Simon Fowler
1992 A&M Records

166 / 167
Almo Sounds Label Sampler (album)
Photography: Mark Higenbottam
1997 Almo Sounds

Sleeper Smart (album)
Photograph supplied by NASA. Digitally remastered by T&CP
1995 Indolent/BMG Records

168 / 169
Redwood Falling Down (single proposal)
Photography: Mark Higenbottam
1997 Almo Sounds

60 Degrees North (range bag & corporate ID)
Photography: Mark Higenbottam
1999 60 Degrees North

170 / 171
Briana Corrigan When My Arms Wrap You Round (album)
Painting: Diarmuid Kelly
1996 East West

Monkey Caving In (single proposal)
Illustration: Andrew Steward
1999 Island Records

Mundy elements from: Pardon Me (single),
To You I Bestow (single), Life's A Cinch (single),
Jelly Legs (album)
Photography: Michael Carsley/Simon Fowler
1996/1997 Epic/Sony Records

172 / 173

180 / 181

188 / 189

196 / 197

174 / 175

182 / 183

190 / 191

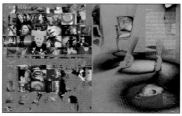

198 / 199

176 / 177

184 / 185

192 / 193

200 / 201

178 / 179

186 / 187

194 / 195

202 / 203

172 / 173
Native Voices Compilation album
Photography: Blinkk
1998 EMI Classics

Hipkiss Bluebird (album)
Photography: Michele Turriani
1997 Sony Records (Germany)

174 / 175
Love And Money Hallelujah Man (single)
Photography: Avid Images
1988 Phonogram/Mercury Records

Love And Money Jocelyn Square (single)
Photography: Avid Images
1988 Phonogram/Mercury Records

Love And Money Strange Kind Of Love (album)
Photography: Avid Images
1988 Phonogram/Mercury Records

Love And Money Strange Kind Of Love (album)
Still-life Photography: Avid Images
1988 Phonogram/Mercury Records

176 / 177
Squeeze Frank (album)
Photography: Trevor Rogers
1989 A&M/Universal Records

Squeeze Cosi Fan Tutti Frutti (album)
Photo-illustration: Simon Fell
1985 A&M/Universal Records

Squeeze No Place Like Home (single)
1985 A&M/Universal Records

Squeeze If It's Love (single)
Photography: Trevor Rogers
1989 A&M/Universal Records

Squeeze Cosi Fan Tutti Frutti En Routti (tour programme)
Photo-illustration: Simon Fell
1985 Squeeze

Squeeze (main image) King George Street (single)
Illustration: Andrew Ekins
1985 A&M/Universal Records

178 / 179
Tears For Fears The Seeds Of Love (album)
Photography: David Scheinmann
1989 Phonogram/Mercury

Tears For Fears Woman In Chains (single)
Photography: David Scheinmann/Avid Images
1989 Phonogram/Mercury Records

Trainspotting Film poster
Photography: Lorenzo Agius
1995 PolyGram Films/Universal

180 / 181
Trainspotting
Photography: Lorenzo Agius
1995 PolyGram Films

182 / 183
Ted Baker Man's Best Friend (in-store poster campaign)
Sally Anne Thompson Animal Photography
1998 Ted Baker

The Brilliant Green Bye Bye Mr Mug (single)
Photography: Julian Quayle
1997 Sony Records Japan

184 / 185
Polly Samson Lying In Bed (book jacket visuals)
Photography: Joseph Hunwick
1999 Polly Samson

Miguel Bosé Bajo El Signo De Cain (album)
Photography: David Scheinmann
1994 Warner Music

186 / 187
Tin Tin Out Eleven To Fly (single poster)
Photography: Simon Fowler
1999 Virgin Records

Patrick Moraz & Bill Bruford Flags (album)
Photography: Gered Mankowitz
1985 EG/Polydor Records

188 / 189
James Seven (album)
Photography: Lennart Nilsson (front cover)
Passportraits: Andrew Ekins
Background illustration: Jane Gott
1992 Phonogram/Mercury Records

Another Country Film poster
Photography: Gered Mankowitz
1984 Virgin Films

190 / 191
Honeycrack Sitting At Home (images from single),
Go Away (single), King Of Misery (single), Prozaic (album)
Photography: Simon Fowler
1995/1996 Sony Records

192 / 193
Greenberry Woods Big Money Item (album)
Photography: Evelyn Hofer
1995 Sire/WEA Records

Greenberry Woods Smash Up (single)
Photography: Evelyn Hofer
1995 Sire/WEA Records

Catatonia Mulder And Scully (single cover image)
Photography: Nigel Schermuly/Cardiff Tourist Office/FTP Digital
1998 Blanco Y Negro Records

194 / 195
Love And Money Dogs In The Traffic (album)
Photography: Nigel Schermuly
1991 Phonogram/Mercury Records

The Darling Buds Tiny Machine (single)
1990 Epic/Sony Records

The Darling Buds Bates (single proposal)
Photography: Simon Fowler
1990 Epic/Sony Records

The Darling Buds Crystal Clear (single)
Photography: Karl Grant
1990 Epic/Sony Records

Jocasta Go (single)
Photography: Michele Turriani
1995 Sony Records

Raw Stylus Pushing Against The Flow (single)
Photography: Phil Knott
1995 Wired Recordings/M&G Records

196 / 197
A Life Less Ordinary Film poster (proposal for teaser campaign)
Photography: Julian Quayle
1997 PolyGram Films

Geri Halliwell Schizophonic (inside and front of album)
Photography: Nick Knight
1999 EMI/Chrysalis Records

198 / 199
Mundy To You I Bestow (single)
1997 Epic/Sony Records

Diesel Park West Shakespeare Alabama (album)
Photography: Trevor Rogers (screenprint by Rob O'Connor/
Karl Scholes) Shakespeare: Mary Evans Picture Library
1989 EMI/Food Records

200 / 201
Stylorouge Video stills
1989-2001

Hipkiss Raw Love (single image)
Photography: Michele Turriani
1997 Sony Records (Germany)

202 / 203
The Blue Nile Saturday Night (single)
Photography: Jeanloup Sieff
1992 Virgin Records

Spear Of Destiny Was That You? (poster for single)
Photography: Anton Corbijn
1987 10/Virgin Records

Pooka Pooka (album back)
Photography: Andy Catlin
1993 WEA Records

Jimi Hendrix The Ultimate Experience (book spreads)
Images on far right by Gered Mankowitz and David Costa
1995 Boxtree

204 / 205

206 / 207

208 / 209

210 / 211

212 / 213

214 / 215

Thank You

To our friends.
To the artists and clients for whom we have worked; photographers and illustrators with whom we have collaborated, those who support us on a daily basis and to all those who have offered their peculiar skills during their time at Stylorouge:

Abby Kyte, Adam Hollywood, Adam Ray, Adrian Boot, Adrian Green, Adrian Peacock, Alan Douglas, Alan McBlane, Alan Parks, Alan (Stan) Kenton, Alan Wood, Alec Byrn, Alessandra Sartore, Alessandra Torri, Alice Lee, Allen Stone, All the photolibraries that have helped us, All our models (human and otherwise), Alonza Bevan, Alison Butler, Alison Wilshaw, Andrew Collins, Andrew Douglas, Andrew Ekins, Andrew Wright, Andy Earl, Andy Farrow, Andy Greatham, Andy Hill, Andy Huckle, Andy Ross, Angie Summerside, Anita Plank, Anne-Marie Lepetre, Anton Corbijn, Antony Wallis, Anuszka Elland, Arnoud Smit, Barbara Tomaszczyk, Barnaby's, Barry Andrews, Blur, Brett Turnbull, Bruno Tilley, Cally Callomon, Cassie Wuta-Ofei, Catherine Davies, Catherine McRae, Carl Rush, Carmine Brudenell, Caroline Diament, Ceri Jones, Charlie Burchill, Chris Bigg, Chris Craske, Chris Difford, Chris Dwyer, Chris Futcher, Chris How, Chris Thomson, Chris Welch, Chrissie Duigh, Cindy Palmano, Claire Allfree, Clare Lusher, Claire O'Brien, Clive Banks, Craig Smith, Craig Tilford, Craig Logan, Crispian Mills, Damon Fisher, Danielle Dax, Dan Weisselberg, Dave Auty, Dave Balfe, David Bower, David Calderley, David Cheek, David Coverdale, David Jones, David Scheinmann, Dean Freeman, Debbie Donovan, Debbie Jones, Deborah Holmes, Dilys Wilde, Dominique Green, Don McCullin, Doug Steward, Duncan Hemphill, DumDums, Ed Holding, Ed Potter, Enya, Elidh McDowall, Elke Leinwand, Elly Plass, Elyse Taylor, Eva Mueller, Eva Zoll, Florence Gravenbeke, FTP Digital, Fran Lima, Frederic Vanhorenbeke, Frog, Gareth Harris, Gavin Evans, Gary Carter, Gary Williams, Ged Doherty, Geoff Brightling, Gered Mankowitz, Gil Gilbert, Graham Lawson, Graham Tucker, Greg Sambrook, Greg Castell, Hambis Charalambous, Helen Walker, Heather McVicar, Henni, Herbie Dayal, Holly Kyte, Holly Warburton, Horacio V Herrera-Richmond, Howard Jones, Ian Brown, Ian Ross, IQ Videographics, Ingrid Robers, Ingrid Western, Jack Soden, James Swinson, Jan & Kenny, Jane Banks, Jane Hilder, Jason Iley, Jason Lamont, Jay Darlington, Jean Garrett, Jean - Paul Goude, Jeff Cottenden, Jenny Buckner, Jez Pearce, Jim Davies, Jim Friedman, Jo Cavanagh, Jo Dunk, Jo Mills, Jo Mirowski, John Bowden, John Butler, John Chuter, John Lay, John Leahy, John Reid, John Wrake, Jon Black, Jeff Veitch, Joseph Hunwick, Julie Wicks, Julia Short, Julia Hormbrey, Julian Gilchrist, Julian Quayle, Justin Crosby, Kampah, Kate (CMO), Karl Grant, Kate Gilchrist, Kathleen Samida, Keiichi Suzuki, Keith Bennett, Kevin Westernberg, Kimberley Bull, Kin Ho, Kit Buckler, Kymber Holt, Liam Hall, Lisa Paulon, Lisa Sowray, Lou De Ville Morel, Louise Robinson, Lo Cole, Louise Constad, Lou de Ville Morel, Lorenzo Agius, Lucy Horton, Mandy Plumb, Maria Van Nouhuys, Matthew Cornford, Marc Lebon, Marcus Tomlinson, Marcus Wilson, Marika Lindgren, Mark Alleyne, Mark Blamire, Mark Caylor, Mark Collen, Mark Fenwick, Mark Higenbottam, Mark Lewis, Mark Thomson, Mark Wood, Martin Gardner, Martin Wade, Martyn Huxford, Martyn Atkins, Michael Ross, Michele Turiani, Mike Bennion, Mike Edwards, Mike McIntyre, Mel Ramos, Mike Putland, Mia Matson, Mick Brownfield, Micky Modern, Mick Harris, Mick Karn, Mick Lowe, Mick Rock, Nancy Gayer, Neil Cavagan, Neil Kirk, Neil Mackintosh, Nels Israelson, Nigel Schermuly, Nic Georgiou, Nick Knight, Nick Haddow, Nick Sherwood, Nick Yates, Nick Ward, Niven Howie, Nova Luxton, Olly Grimwood, Paddy McAloon, Panni Charrington, Paul Allan, Paul Cox, Paul Postle, Paul Young, Paul Winterhart, Paula Keenan, Pearl O'Connor, Peter Anderson, Phillida Bannister, Phil Jude, Phil and Keith at Kitchenware, Polly Miller, Ray Kyte, Rebecca La Porta, Rian Hughes, Richard Beeching, Richard Bull, Richard Engler, Richard Haughton, Rick Mann, Rob Marron, Rob Mills x2, Rob Chenery, Robert Klanten, Roma and Nicky Ryan, Roma Martyniuk, Romaine Campbell, Rose Harrison, Rupert Style, Rusty Egan, Russell Young, Ryan Jones, Ryoji Oba, Sandie Shaw, Sarah Clayman, Shazzy Thomas, Sheila Rock, Sheridan Wall, Siena Jakobi, Simon Bull, Simon Conroy, Simon Fell, Simon Fowler and Nicky Longley, Simon Scarborough, Simone Fischer, Squeeze, Stella Onigade, Steve Abbott, Steve O'Neil, Steve Bendell, Steve Luxford, Steve Davis, Stev & Sari, Straw, Stuart Douglas, Stuart Mackenzie, Sue Lacy, Suzette Newman, Suzy Koo, Taeko Onuki, Takashi Homma, Takeshi Maeda, Tamar, Tansy Spinks, Tapestry MM, Tammy Tipper, Terry Felgate, The Lonely Goats, Thomi Wroblewski, Tim Harrison, Tim O'Donnell, Tim Simmonds, Tommy Steele, Tony Hung, Tony King, Tony McGuinness, Tony Wadsworth, Trevor Rogers, Trevor Wyatt, Tris Penna, Victoria Pearson-Cameron, Vicky Wickham, Viv Mabon, Wayne Robinson, Will King, Willy Richardson, Zed Nelson, ZEFA, Zoe Kyte,
Finally (as I once read on the credits of an album) to anyone we may have forgotten; blame our heads not our hearts.

Contributors

Jim Davies is a writer and cultural commentator. His work has appeared in specialist design and advertising titles including Eye, Print, Campaign and Ray Gun as well as the Guardian, Daily Telegraph, Financial Times and Sunday Times Magazine. He is author of The Book of Guinness Advertising and Royal Mail's Year Books (The Stories Behind the Stamps) for 1999, 2000 and 2001 – plus the first chapter of several novels. He lives in Warwickshire with his wife and two young sons, where he listens to a lot of Al Green.

Andrew Collins Raised in Northampton, inspired at Chelsea School Of Art and corrupted at the NME during the so-called Acid House /Madchester years, Andrew has since discovered an assortment of ways to fulfil his need to show off, including amateur dramatics (he co-wrote plays with Harry Hill before he was Harry Hill), radio (he won a Sony Award for Radio 1's Collins & Maconie's Hit Parade in 1995) and now television, writing for EastEnders and appearing on anything they'll let him appear on. He has been the editor of Q and Empire, wrote Billy Bragg's official biography Still Suitable For Miners and annually attempts to inspire students at the NUS Media Conference in London. He currently presents Radio 4's weekly movie show Back Row.

Claire Allfree Feature writer on London Metro, Claire graduated from Cambridge and is a journalist specializing in music, books and theatre, offering her the opportunity to combine her career with her abiding passions. Outside this she has no life at all.

204 / 205
The Creatures Miss The Girl (single)
Photography: Gil Gilbert
1983 Polydor Records

The Creatures Feast (album)
Photography: Gil Gilbert
1983 Polydor Records

Hipkiss Raw Love (proposed image for single)
Photography: Michele Turriani
1997 Sony Records (Germany)

206 / 207
Menswear Being Brave (single poster)
Photography: Simon Fowler
1996 London/Laurel Records

208 / 209
Prefab Sprout Andromeda Heights (album)
Illustration: Anne Magill
1997 Columbia Records

Background:
Island Sampler (Image from front of CD)
Photography: Tony Hung
1999 Island/Universal Records

It Proposal for corporate ID
1990 Dave Balfe/Mike Edwards

Usura Open Your Mind (album)
Photography: David Scheinmann
Deconstruction Records

It proposal for House Bag record packaging

210
Excellent Cadavers/Falcone Proposal for film poster
Illustration: Mark Higenbottam
1998 HBO Pictures

211
Falcone
Illustration: Carl Rush
1998 HBO Pictures

212 / 213
Octopus From A To B (album)
Illustration: Mick Brownfield (main)/Rian Hughes (below)
1996 EMI/Food Records

Playlouder Corporate ID/Launch Party Invite
2000 AML/Playlouder

214 / 215
Hydra Corporate ID
1999 Regal/EMI Records

Lisa Stansfield Face Up (album proposal)
Photography: Eva Mueller
2001 Arista Records

223
Rob O'Connor and Dr John
Photography: Andy Earl
1998

Inside flap, front cover: Cover Photography by Takashi Homma

Scanning by FTP Digital
Photographic prints by Tapestry MM and The Image

Delicious
the design and art direction of Stylorouge
by Rob O'Connor

Book design by Stylorouge.
All designs by Stylorouge.
©1980-2001 Stylorouge except:
Ronny: If You Want Me To Stay (single); Sham
69: The First, The Best And The Last (album);
Siouxsie And The Banshees: Spellbound
(poster); Israel (single), Christine (single); The
Chords, So Far Away (album), Maybe
Tomorrow (single); The Passions, I'm In Love
With A German Film Star (single); The
Wanderers, Only Lovers Left Alive (album);
designed by Rob O'Connor, ©1980/1981
Polydor Records; Geri Halliwell: logo ©2000
Geri Productions; Rolling Stones: No Security
(album) ©1998 Rolling Stones; Pink Floyd logo
©1994 Pink Floyd.

Cover photography by Takashi Homma

Scanning by FTP Colour Imaging
Photographic prints by Tapestry MM
and The Image

Die Deutsche Bibliothek-CIP Einheitsaufnahme
O'Connor, Rob:
Delicious : the design and art direction of
Stylorouge / Rob O'Connor
Hrsg.: Robert Klanten. - Berlin :
Die Gestalten-Verl., 2001
ISBN 3-931126-49-8

Printed by Medialis Offset, Berlin
Made in Europe

For your local dgv distributor please check out:
www.die-gestalten.de